JADEN CROSS

DynamoDB and PostgreSQL for RESTful API Development

Contents

What is a RESTful API?

I n the realm of software development, particularly in the context of web services, the term RESTful API has become a foundational concept. REST, which stands for Representational State Transfer, is an architectural style that dictates how web services should be designed, implemented, and consumed. An API, or Application Programming Interface, acts as a bridge allowing different software applications to communicate with one another. Together, REST and APIs form a powerful toolset for building scalable, efficient, and easy-to-use web services.

Understanding REST

To fully grasp what a RESTful API is, it's essential to understand the principles of REST. REST was introduced by Roy Fielding in his doctoral dissertation in 2000. It provides a set of guidelines and constraints for creating stateless, client-server communication, which enhances the performance and scalability of web services.

Key principles of REST include:

- **Statelessness**: In RESTful architecture, each request from a client contains all the information needed for the server to fulfill that request. The server does not store any client context between requests. This statelessness simplifies the server design and improves scalability since it doesn't need to manage session states.

- **Client-Server Architecture**: REST separates the user interface from the data storage. This separation allows the client and server to evolve independently. A client can interact with a server through standardized requests, while the server manages the data and business logic.

- **Uniform Interface**: RESTful services have a uniform interface that simplifies interactions. This includes standard methods like GET, POST, PUT, DELETE, and the use of URIs (Uniform Resource Identifiers) to uniquely identify resources. This uniformity makes it easier for developers to understand and use the API.

- **Resource-Based**: REST emphasizes resources rather than actions. Resources can be any type of object or entity, such as users, products, or services. Each resource is identified by a unique URI, and clients interact with these resources through standard HTTP methods.

- **Representations**: Resources can have multiple representations. A resource can be represented in various formats, such as JSON, XML, or HTML. When a client requests a resource, the server sends back the appropriate representation based on the client's requirements.

- **Caching**: Responses from the server can be explicitly marked as cacheable or non-cacheable. This caching mechanism can reduce the number of requests made to the server, improving performance and efficiency.

The Role of APIs

An **API** serves as a set of rules and protocols that allow different software applications to communicate with one another. In the context of RESTful APIs, it provides developers with a standard way to interact with web services over the Internet.

APIs can be categorized into several types, including:

- **Web APIs**: These APIs are designed for use over the web and follow standard protocols like HTTP. RESTful APIs are a subset of web APIs.

- **Library APIs**: These APIs allow developers to interact with software libraries or frameworks directly within their code.

- **Operating System APIs**: These APIs enable applications to interact with the underlying operating system, accessing system resources and functionalities.

RESTful APIs are particularly popular due to their simplicity, scalability, and flexibility. They enable developers to build applications that can easily interact with other services, retrieve data, and perform operations in a standardized manner.

Characteristics of RESTful APIs

RESTful APIs exhibit several key characteristics that make them appealing for modern web development:

- **Simplicity**: RESTful APIs use standard HTTP methods, which are familiar to most developers. This simplicity allows for easier integration and adoption.
- **Scalability**: The stateless nature of REST allows for easy scaling of services. Servers can handle more requests without maintaining state information for each client.
- **Interoperability**: RESTful APIs can be consumed by any client that understands HTTP. This makes them platform-agnostic and allows for seamless integration between diverse systems.
- **Flexibility**: RESTful APIs can return data in various formats, such as JSON or XML, depending on client needs. This flexibility allows developers to choose the most suitable representation for their applications.
- **Versioning**: RESTful APIs can be versioned easily, allowing developers to introduce new features or changes without disrupting existing clients. Versioning can be managed through the URI or HTTP headers.

HTTP Methods and Status Codes

RESTful APIs rely heavily on standard HTTP methods to perform actions on resources. The most commonly used methods include:

- **GET**: Retrieve a resource or a collection of resources. For example, a GET request to /users might return a list of users, while a GET request to /users/1 would return the details of a specific user.
- **POST**: Create a new resource. A POST request to /users with user data in the request body would create a new user.

- **PUT**: Update an existing resource. A PUT request to /users/1 with updated user data would modify the user with ID 1.
- **DELETE**: Remove a resource. A DELETE request to /users/1 would delete the user with ID 1.

In addition to HTTP methods, status codes play a critical role in RESTful API communication. They provide feedback about the success or failure of requests. Some common status codes include:

- **200 OK**: The request was successful.
- **201 Created**: A resource was successfully created.
- **204 No Content**: The request was successful, but there is no content to return.
- **400 Bad Request**: The server could not understand the request due to invalid syntax.
- **404 Not Found**: The requested resource was not found.
- **500 Internal Server Error**: The server encountered an error while processing the request.

Designing a RESTful API

Designing a RESTful API involves several considerations to ensure usability, maintainability, and scalability. Here are some key design principles:

- **Use Meaningful URIs**: URIs should be intuitive and represent the resource they point to. For example, /api/v1/users is more descriptive than /api/v1/item123.
- **Follow RESTful Conventions**: Adhere to RESTful conventions regarding resource naming and HTTP methods. For example, use plural nouns for resource names and leverage appropriate HTTP methods for CRUD operations.
- **Document the API**: Comprehensive documentation is essential for developers who will be using the API. Include details about endpoints,

request parameters, response formats, and example usage.

- **Implement Authentication and Authorization**: Secure your API by implementing authentication mechanisms (such as OAuth or API keys) and ensuring that users have appropriate permissions to access resources.
- **Version Your API**: Use versioning in your URIs (e.g., /api/v1/) to manage changes and maintain backward compatibility as the API evolves.
- **Enable CORS**: Cross-Origin Resource Sharing (CORS) allows resources to be requested from different domains. Configuring CORS appropriately enhances the usability of your API across different platforms.

Common Use Cases for RESTful APIs

RESTful APIs are widely used across various applications and industries. Some common use cases include:

- **Web Applications**: Most modern web applications rely on RESTful APIs to communicate with back-end services, retrieve data, and update content dynamically.
- **Mobile Applications**: Mobile apps often use RESTful APIs to access server resources, synchronize data, and perform user interactions.
- **Microservices Architecture**: In microservices, individual services communicate with each other using RESTful APIs, allowing for loose coupling and easier management of complex systems.
- **Internet of Things (IoT)**: RESTful APIs are employed in IoT devices to facilitate communication between devices, servers, and cloud services.
- **Third-Party Integrations**: Many platforms provide RESTful APIs to allow developers to integrate their services, enabling functionality like payment processing, social media sharing, or data analysis.

RESTful APIs are an essential part of modern web development, enabling seamless communication between clients and servers. Their adherence to

REST principles ensures that they are simple, scalable, and flexible, making them a preferred choice for developers across various domains. As you delve deeper into this book, you will explore how to effectively design, implement, and leverage RESTful APIs using DynamoDB and PostgreSQL, gaining insights into best practices, advanced techniques, and real-world applications.

Principles of REST

Understanding the principles of REST (Representational State Transfer) is crucial for anyone involved in developing, designing, or consuming RESTful APIs. These principles establish the foundation for creating scalable, efficient, and maintainable web services. Below, we delve into the core principles of REST that guide its architecture.

Statelessness

One of the defining characteristics of RESTful architecture is its stateless-ness. Each client request must contain all the information the server needs to fulfill that request. This means that the server does not store any session state or context between requests. Each interaction is treated independently.

Implications of Statelessness:

- **Scalability**: Since the server does not have to maintain session information, it can easily scale to handle a large number of concurrent requests. Load balancers can distribute requests to different servers without concern for client session data.
- **Simplicity**: Statelessness simplifies server design and implementation. Developers can focus on building a reliable API without the complexity of managing sessions or user states.
- **Reliability**: In a stateless architecture, if a server fails, clients can simply retry their requests on another server without any loss of context.

Statelessness does not mean that the client does not maintain state; it simply means that any state management required by the client is handled on the client side, not by the server.

Client-Server Architecture

REST is built on a client-server architecture that separates the client (the user interface) from the server (the data storage and business logic). This separation allows both the client and server to evolve independently, which is beneficial for several reasons:

- **Separation of Concerns**: Developers can work on the client-side user interface independently of the server-side data management. This enables more focused development efforts and improves maintainability.
- **Interoperability**: Clients can interact with any server that adheres to the RESTful API standards, regardless of the underlying technology stack. This flexibility allows for a wide range of client applications, from web browsers to mobile apps and IoT devices.
- **Ease of Updates**: Since the client and server are decoupled, either can be updated without requiring changes to the other. For instance, a new version of the client can be deployed without altering the server, as long as the API remains consistent.

This principle promotes a more modular and adaptable approach to application design.

Uniform Interface

The concept of a uniform interface is central to REST architecture. It simplifies interactions between the client and server, enabling developers to build APIs that are intuitive and easy to use. A uniform interface encompasses several constraints:

- **Resource Identification**: Resources are identified using URIs (Uniform Resource Identifiers). Each resource is accessible via a unique URI, making it easy for clients to locate and interact with it. For example, the URI /api/v1/users might refer to the collection of user resources.
- **Standardized Methods**: RESTful APIs use standard HTTP methods

to perform actions on resources:

- **GET**: Retrieve a representation of a resource.
- **POST**: Create a new resource.
- **PUT**: Update an existing resource.
- **DELETE**: Remove a resource.
- This standardization means developers can predict how to interact with the API without needing to learn custom methods.
- **Resource Representation**: Resources can have multiple representations, such as JSON or XML. When a client requests a resource, the server can return the representation in the format specified by the client's request headers.

By adhering to these constraints, RESTful APIs achieve a uniform interface that simplifies development and improves usability.

Resource-Based Architecture

In REST, the focus is on resources rather than actions. This resource-oriented approach encourages developers to model their APIs around the entities they are working with. Each resource represents a specific object or entity within the system, such as a user, product, or order.

Characteristics of Resource-Based Architecture:

- **Resource URIs**: Each resource is represented by a URI, which uniquely identifies it. This allows clients to access, create, update, or delete resources through their respective URIs.
- **CRUD Operations**: Clients interact with resources using standard CRUD (Create, Read, Update, Delete) operations, which map to HTTP methods (POST, GET, PUT, DELETE). This clear mapping makes it easier for developers to understand and use the API.
- **Hierarchical Structure**: Resources can have a hierarchical structure, enabling the organization of related resources. For example, a collection of orders might be represented as /api/v1/users/1/orders, indicating that these orders belong to the user with ID 1.

This resource-based architecture enhances clarity and provides a logical framework for organizing and accessing data.

Representations

RESTful APIs allow resources to have multiple representations. When a client requests a resource, it can specify the desired representation format in the request headers (e.g., Accept: application/json). The server responds with the resource in the requested format, allowing clients to choose the representation that best suits their needs.

Implications of Resource Representations:

- **Flexibility**: Clients can consume data in various formats, which is particularly useful in diverse environments where different technologies may be in use.
- **Interoperability**: By supporting multiple representations, RESTful APIs can cater to a wide range of clients, from web browsers to mobile applications and IoT devices.
- **Media Types**: RESTful APIs utilize media types (MIME types) to indicate the format of the data being sent or received. Common media types include application/json, application/xml, and text/html. This use of media types enhances the API's ability to communicate effectively with clients.

Caching

Caching is an essential principle in RESTful architecture that improves performance and reduces latency. By allowing responses to be cached, RESTful APIs can minimize the number of requests made to the server, leading to faster response times and reduced load.

Key Aspects of Caching in REST:

- **Cacheable Responses**: Responses from the server can be marked as cacheable or non-cacheable. Caching can be implemented using HTTP headers such as Cache-Control and Expires, which instruct clients and intermediary proxies on how to handle cached responses.

- **Improved Performance**: Caching can significantly enhance the performance of web applications. For frequently requested resources, clients can retrieve cached responses without contacting the server, leading to faster load times.
- **Consistency**: Developers must consider the implications of caching on data consistency. Strategies like cache invalidation and cache expiration help ensure that clients receive up-to-date information when needed.

Layered System

RESTful architecture promotes a layered system where different layers of the application can interact with one another without being tightly coupled. This layered approach enhances scalability, security, and maintainability.

Benefits of Layered Systems:

- **Scalability**: By decoupling components into layers, each layer can be scaled independently. For example, a load balancer can distribute requests among multiple servers without affecting the application logic.
- **Security**: Security measures can be applied at different layers, protecting sensitive data while maintaining access controls. For instance, authentication and authorization can be handled by a dedicated layer, isolating security concerns from the business logic.
- **Intermediary Services**: Layered systems allow for the introduction of intermediary services, such as caching servers or proxy servers, which can enhance performance and provide additional functionalities.

Code on Demand (Optional)

While not a requirement for REST, the principle of **code on demand** allows servers to extend client functionality by transferring executable code. This can include scripts or applets that clients can execute. However, this principle is rarely used in practice due to potential security issues and increased complexity.

The principles of REST form the backbone of RESTful APIs, guiding developers in creating efficient, scalable, and user-friendly web services. By adhering to these principles, developers can ensure that their APIs are easy to use, maintain, and extend over time. Understanding and implementing these principles will not only enhance the quality of your API design but also contribute to a more seamless experience for users and developers alike.

As we progress through this book, we will explore how to apply these principles effectively in the context of using DynamoDB and PostgreSQL for RESTful API development, ensuring that you are well-equipped to build robust and efficient applications.

Common Use Cases for RESTful APIs

RESTful APIs have become integral to modern application development due to their versatility and ease of integration. They are employed across various domains and industries, facilitating communication between clients and servers in a structured and efficient manner. Below, we explore some of the most common use cases for RESTful APIs, highlighting their practical applications and benefits.

Web Applications

Web applications are among the most prevalent use cases for RESTful APIs. They enable dynamic content updates and seamless interactions between the client-side interface and server-side resources. Key characteristics include:

- **Data Retrieval**: RESTful APIs allow web applications to retrieve data from servers in real-time. For example, a news website can use an API to fetch the latest articles without requiring a full page refresh. This creates a smoother user experience.
- **Form Submissions**: Web applications often require users to submit forms, such as login credentials or registration data. RESTful APIs handle these submissions by sending data to the server using POST requests and returning responses based on the outcome.

- **Single Page Applications (SPAs)**: Frameworks like React, Angular, and Vue.js leverage RESTful APIs to create SPAs that load content dynamically. By using APIs, SPAs can efficiently manage application states and enhance user interactions without the need for constant page reloads.

Mobile Applications

The rise of mobile applications has further driven the adoption of RESTful APIs. Mobile apps typically need to communicate with back-end services for various functions, such as user authentication, data storage, and remote interactions. Key points include:

- **Data Synchronization**: Mobile apps often need to synchronize data with remote servers. RESTful APIs facilitate this process by enabling apps to fetch updated data and push local changes back to the server, ensuring users have access to the latest information.
- **User Authentication**: Mobile applications frequently require user authentication, which can be efficiently handled through RESTful APIs. Users can log in via API calls, and authentication tokens can be used for subsequent requests, ensuring secure access.
- **Location-Based Services**: Many mobile apps offer location-based features, such as finding nearby restaurants or services. RESTful APIs can provide location data by querying databases and returning results tailored to the user's geographic location.

Microservices Architecture

RESTful APIs are a natural fit for microservices architectures, where applications are built as a collection of loosely coupled services. This architectural style offers several advantages:

- **Service Independence**: Each microservice can expose its functionality through a RESTful API, allowing other services or clients to interact with it independently. This modularity enables teams to work on different services simultaneously, accelerating development.

- **Inter-Service Communication**: Microservices can communicate with one another through RESTful APIs, allowing them to share data and invoke functionality across the system. This promotes flexibility and scalability, as services can be deployed and updated independently.
- **Technology Diversity**: Different microservices can be developed using different programming languages or frameworks. As long as they expose a consistent RESTful API, they can interoperate seamlessly.

Internet of Things (IoT)

The Internet of Things (IoT) is another area where RESTful APIs play a crucial role. With the proliferation of connected devices, RESTful APIs provide a means for devices to communicate with servers and each other. Key applications include:

- **Device Management**: RESTful APIs enable the management of IoT devices, allowing users to register, configure, and monitor devices remotely. For example, smart home devices can communicate with a central server via RESTful APIs to update their status or receive commands.
- **Data Collection and Analytics**: IoT devices generate vast amounts of data that can be collected and analyzed. RESTful APIs allow devices to send data to cloud services for processing, enabling real-time analytics and insights.
- **Remote Control**: Many IoT applications require remote control capabilities. RESTful APIs can facilitate this by allowing users to send commands to devices from anywhere with an internet connection.

Third-Party Integrations

RESTful APIs are essential for enabling third-party integrations, allowing developers to extend the functionality of their applications by connecting to external services. Common use cases include:

- **Payment Processing**: E-commerce platforms often integrate with payment gateways using RESTful APIs. This allows for secure transactions and the management of payment processing without requiring extensive in-house development.
- **Social Media Integration**: Many applications provide options for users to log in or share content via social media platforms. RESTful APIs enable this integration by allowing applications to authenticate users and post updates directly to social media accounts.
- **Data Enrichment**: Applications can enhance their features by integrating with data providers via RESTful APIs. For example, a travel booking application can leverage APIs from weather services to provide users with relevant weather forecasts for their travel destinations.

Cloud Services

Cloud computing platforms heavily rely on RESTful APIs to provide services to developers and users. These APIs enable the management of cloud resources and facilitate seamless interactions. Key aspects include:

- **Resource Provisioning**: Developers can provision and manage cloud resources (e.g., virtual machines, databases) through RESTful APIs. This allows for automated scaling, resource allocation, and infrastructure management.
- **Data Storage**: Cloud storage solutions often expose RESTful APIs for users to upload, download, and manage files. For instance, Amazon S3 (Simple Storage Service) provides a RESTful API for object storage, allowing developers to integrate cloud storage capabilities into their applications.
- **Analytics and Monitoring**: Cloud services provide RESTful APIs for monitoring performance, accessing analytics, and managing application health. Developers can use these APIs to gather insights and automate responses to changing conditions.

Content Management Systems (CMS)

Content management systems (CMS) often utilize RESTful APIs to provide flexibility and facilitate interactions with content. Key applications include:

- **Content Retrieval**: RESTful APIs allow web applications to fetch content from a CMS dynamically. This enables developers to create custom front-ends that can pull content based on specific user interactions or preferences.
- **Content Updates**: RESTful APIs enable users to create, update, and delete content from the CMS programmatically. This allows for automated content management workflows and integration with other services.
- **User Management**: Many CMS platforms use RESTful APIs to manage user accounts, permissions, and roles. This allows for fine-grained access control and integration with external authentication systems.

Data-Driven Applications

Data-driven applications, which rely heavily on dynamic data interactions, benefit significantly from RESTful APIs. Key features include:

- **Real-Time Data Updates**: Applications that require real-time data updates can leverage RESTful APIs to fetch the latest data as needed. For example, stock trading platforms use APIs to pull live stock prices and trading information.
- **Data Visualization**: Applications that present data visually often use RESTful APIs to retrieve the data needed for charts, graphs, and dashboards. This enables users to interact with and analyze data in a meaningful way.
- **Reporting and Analytics**: RESTful APIs can facilitate the generation of reports and analytics by allowing applications to access raw data and present it in user-friendly formats.

The versatility of RESTful APIs makes them an ideal choice for a wide range of applications and use cases. From web and mobile applications to IoT devices and cloud services, RESTful APIs provide the foundation for seamless communication and interaction between clients and servers. As we continue through this book, we will delve into how to effectively implement RESTful APIs using DynamoDB and PostgreSQL, ensuring you are equipped to leverage these powerful tools in your development projects.

Overview of Database Choices for API Development

When designing a RESTful API, selecting the right database is crucial for ensuring optimal performance, scalability, and maintainability. The choice of database directly affects how data is managed, accessed, and manipulated, impacting the overall efficiency of the API. This section provides an overview of the primary database options available for API development, highlighting their characteristics, strengths, and weaknesses.

Relational Databases

Relational databases have been a staple in data management for decades. They store data in structured formats using tables, which consist of rows and columns. The relationships between tables are established through foreign keys, allowing for complex queries and data integrity.

Key Features:

- **Structured Query Language (SQL)**: Relational databases utilize SQL for querying and managing data. SQL provides powerful capabilities for data manipulation, including complex joins, aggregations, and subqueries.
- **ACID Compliance**: Relational databases adhere to the ACID (Atomicity, Consistency, Isolation, Durability) properties, ensuring reliable transactions and data integrity.
- **Data Integrity**: The use of foreign keys and constraints helps maintain data integrity, preventing invalid data entries and ensuring relationships between entities are respected.

Popular Relational Databases:

- **PostgreSQL**: An advanced open-source relational database known for its extensibility, support for complex queries, and strong adherence to standards. PostgreSQL is an excellent choice for applications requiring complex data models and high data integrity.
- **MySQL**: A widely used open-source relational database known for its speed and ease of use. MySQL is suitable for a variety of applications, especially web applications and small to medium-sized projects.

Use Cases for Relational Databases:

- Applications requiring complex transactions and strong data consistency.
- Systems with well-defined data schemas, such as e-commerce platforms, financial applications, and content management systems.

NoSQL Databases

NoSQL databases emerged to address the limitations of relational databases, particularly in handling unstructured data and scaling horizontally. They provide a flexible schema, allowing for the storage of various data types, including JSON, XML, and key-value pairs.

Key Features:

- **Flexible Schema**: NoSQL databases allow for dynamic schemas, enabling developers to modify the structure of stored data without downtime. This flexibility is beneficial in environments where data requirements evolve rapidly.
- **Horizontal Scalability**: Many NoSQL databases are designed to scale horizontally, allowing them to handle increased loads by distributing data across multiple servers. This makes them ideal for applications with high traffic and large datasets.
- **Variety of Data Models**: NoSQL databases come in several types,

including document stores, key-value stores, column-family stores, and graph databases, each optimized for specific use cases.

Popular NoSQL Databases:

- **MongoDB**: A widely-used document store that stores data in JSON-like BSON (Binary JSON) format. MongoDB is particularly suited for applications requiring high write loads, flexible data structures, and fast read operations.
- **DynamoDB**: A fully managed key-value and document database provided by Amazon Web Services (AWS). DynamoDB is known for its high availability, low latency, and automatic scaling, making it an excellent choice for applications with unpredictable workloads.

Use Cases for NoSQL Databases:

- Applications dealing with large volumes of unstructured or semi-structured data, such as social media platforms, big data analytics, and content delivery networks.
- Real-time applications requiring quick read and write operations, such as gaming applications and IoT systems.

In-Memory Databases

In-memory databases store data in the main memory (RAM) rather than on disk, allowing for extremely fast data access and processing. They are particularly useful for applications that require real-time performance and low latency.

Key Features:

- **Speed**: In-memory databases can deliver response times in microseconds, making them ideal for high-performance applications.
- **Data Persistence Options**: Many in-memory databases provide options for data persistence, allowing data to be saved to disk for

durability while still benefiting from in-memory speeds.

Popular In-Memory Databases:

- **Redis**: An open-source in-memory key-value store known for its speed and support for various data structures (e.g., strings, hashes, lists). Redis is commonly used for caching, session management, and real-time analytics.
- **Memcached**: A high-performance distributed memory caching system used to speed up dynamic web applications by alleviating database load.

Use Cases for In-Memory Databases:

- Applications requiring low-latency data access, such as financial trading platforms and real-time analytics dashboards.
- Caching solutions to enhance the performance of web applications by storing frequently accessed data in memory.

Graph Databases

Graph databases are designed to handle highly interconnected data by using graph structures (nodes, edges, and properties) to represent and store data. They excel at managing relationships and can efficiently execute complex queries involving traversals.

Key Features:

- **Relationship-Centric**: Graph databases focus on the relationships between data points, making them suitable for applications with intricate relationship mappings.
- **Flexible Schema**: Graph databases allow for flexible schemas, enabling developers to adapt the data model as relationships evolve.

Popular Graph Databases:

- **Neo4j**: A leading graph database known for its ability to handle complex queries and large datasets. Neo4j uses a property graph model, allowing for rich data representation.
- **Amazon Neptune**: A fully managed graph database service that supports both property graphs and RDF (Resource Description Framework) graph models.

Use Cases for Graph Databases:

- Applications requiring deep relationship analysis, such as social networks, recommendation engines, and fraud detection systems.
- Content management systems that rely on tagging and categorizing content based on relationships.

Choosing the Right Database for Your API

When selecting a database for your RESTful API, consider the following factors:

- **Data Structure**: Evaluate the nature of your data. If you have well-defined, structured data, a relational database may be suitable. If you anticipate changes in data structure or need to handle unstructured data, consider a NoSQL database.
- **Scalability Requirements**: Assess your application's scalability needs. If you expect rapid growth in data volume or traffic, choose a database that can scale horizontally, such as NoSQL or in-memory databases.
- **Performance Needs**: Determine the performance requirements of your application. For low-latency requirements, consider in-memory databases. For complex transactions, relational databases may be the best choice.
- **Development Team Expertise**: Consider your development team's familiarity with various database technologies. Opt for a database that aligns with your team's skill set to streamline development and maintenance.

- **Integration Considerations**: Ensure that the chosen database can easily integrate with your API framework and other technologies in your stack.

The choice of database is a critical decision when developing a RESTful API. Each database type—whether relational, NoSQL, in-memory, or graph—has its strengths and weaknesses, and understanding these can guide you in making the right selection for your application's needs. As you move forward in this book, we will explore how to leverage both DynamoDB and PostgreSQL effectively in your RESTful API development, focusing on practical applications, best practices, and performance optimization strategies.

Introuction to DynamoDB

O**verview of DynamoDB**
Amazon DynamoDB is a fully managed NoSQL database service offered by Amazon Web Services (AWS). Designed to provide high availability, scalability, and low-latency performance, DynamoDB is ideal for applications that require quick access to large volumes of data. This section provides a comprehensive overview of DynamoDB, covering its architecture, key features, use cases, and advantages.

Understanding DynamoDB

DynamoDB was developed to address the challenges of managing data at scale. It is a distributed database that allows for seamless horizontal scaling, meaning it can handle large amounts of data and traffic without compromising performance. Its architecture is built around several core concepts:

- **Tables**: Data in DynamoDB is organized into tables, which are analogous to tables in relational databases. Each table is identified by a unique name and consists of items.
- **Items**: An item is a single record in a DynamoDB table. Each item is composed of attributes, which are the data fields within that item. Items in DynamoDB are similar to rows in relational databases, but they can vary in structure, allowing for flexible data modeling.
- **Attributes**: Attributes are the individual data elements that make up an item. Each attribute has a name and a data type, such as string, number,

binary, Boolean, or set.

- **Primary Keys**: Every item in a DynamoDB table is uniquely identified by a primary key. DynamoDB supports two types of primary keys:
- **Partition Key**: A single attribute that uniquely identifies each item in the table. The partition key is hashed to determine the item's location in the distributed system.
- **Composite Key**: A combination of a partition key and a sort key. The partition key groups items, while the sort key allows for multiple items within the same partition, providing a way to sort and filter data.
- **Indexes**: DynamoDB supports secondary indexes, which allow for efficient querying of data based on attributes other than the primary key. There are two types of secondary indexes:
- **Global Secondary Index (GSI)**: An index with a partition key and an optional sort key that can be different from those of the base table. GSIs allow for queries on non-key attributes.
- **Local Secondary Index (LSI)**: An index that has the same partition key as the base table but a different sort key. LSIs enable queries based on alternate sorting options within the same partition.

Key Features of DynamoDB

DynamoDB offers a range of features that make it a powerful choice for developers looking to build scalable applications:

- **Fully Managed Service**: As a fully managed database, DynamoDB handles infrastructure provisioning, software patching, and scaling automatically. This allows developers to focus on building their applications without worrying about database management tasks.
- **Automatic Scaling**: DynamoDB automatically scales throughput capacity to accommodate varying workloads. Developers can define minimum and maximum capacity limits, and DynamoDB adjusts to meet application demands, ensuring consistent performance.
- **Low Latency**: DynamoDB is designed for single-digit millisecond response times, making it suitable for real-time applications. Its

performance is consistent, regardless of the amount of data stored or the number of requests made.

- **Global Availability**: DynamoDB is a global service, allowing developers to create tables in multiple AWS regions. This ensures high availability and low-latency access to data from anywhere in the world.
- **Event-Driven Architecture**: DynamoDB integrates with AWS Lambda, enabling event-driven programming. Developers can create triggers to automatically respond to changes in DynamoDB tables, such as adding new items or updating existing ones.
- **Fine-Grained Access Control**: DynamoDB provides robust security features, including AWS Identity and Access Management (IAM) for fine-grained access control. Developers can define permissions for individual actions on tables, items, and attributes, ensuring that only authorized users can access sensitive data.
- **Backup and Restore**: DynamoDB offers built-in backup and restore capabilities, allowing developers to create on-demand backups of their tables and restore them as needed. This ensures data durability and protection against accidental deletions.
- **Streams**: DynamoDB Streams capture changes to items in a table, providing a time-ordered sequence of item modifications. This feature allows developers to build applications that react to data changes, such as sending notifications or triggering workflows.

Use Cases for DynamoDB

DynamoDB is well-suited for a variety of applications and use cases, including:

- **Web and Mobile Applications**: Many web and mobile applications use DynamoDB to store user data, session information, and application state. Its low-latency performance makes it an excellent choice for applications with high traffic and real-time requirements.
- **Gaming Applications**: Online gaming platforms often use DynamoDB to manage player profiles, game state, and leaderboards. Its ability

to handle large volumes of concurrent reads and writes is ideal for maintaining game performance.

- **IoT Applications**: Internet of Things (IoT) applications generate massive amounts of data from connected devices. DynamoDB can store and process this data in real-time, enabling analytics and monitoring.
- **E-commerce Platforms**: DynamoDB is commonly used in e-commerce applications to manage product catalogs, user carts, and order history. Its scalability ensures that it can handle peak traffic during sales events.
- **Content Management Systems (CMS)**: Many CMS platforms leverage DynamoDB to store articles, user-generated content, and metadata. Its flexible data model allows for varying content structures and easy retrieval.

Advantages of DynamoDB

DynamoDB offers several advantages that make it an attractive choice for developers:

- **Scalability**: DynamoDB's automatic scaling capabilities allow it to handle unpredictable workloads, making it suitable for applications with variable traffic patterns.
- **Cost-Effectiveness**: With a pay-as-you-go pricing model, developers only pay for the resources they consume. This flexibility allows for cost-effective management of workloads.
- **Easy Integration with AWS Services**: As part of the AWS ecosystem, DynamoDB integrates seamlessly with other AWS services such as Lambda, API Gateway, and S3. This integration simplifies the development of serverless architectures and microservices.
- **High Availability and Durability**: DynamoDB replicates data across multiple availability zones, ensuring high availability and durability. This redundancy protects against data loss and downtime.
- **Support for Multiple Data Models**: DynamoDB's support for both document and key-value data models allows developers to choose the

most suitable approach for their application needs.

Amazon DynamoDB is a powerful and flexible NoSQL database service that excels in scalability, performance, and ease of use. Its fully managed nature allows developers to focus on building applications without the overhead of database management. With features such as automatic scaling, low-latency access, and seamless integration with other AWS services, DynamoDB is well-equipped to handle a wide range of applications—from web and mobile apps to IoT solutions and beyond.

As we proceed through this book, we will explore how to effectively use DynamoDB in conjunction with RESTful API development, focusing on practical examples, best practices, and optimization techniques to ensure your applications achieve peak performance and reliability.

Key Features and Advantages of DynamoDB

Amazon DynamoDB is designed to meet the demands of modern applications that require high performance, scalability, and flexibility. Its architecture and features cater to a wide range of use cases, making it a popular choice among developers. This section explores the key features and advantages of DynamoDB, highlighting how they contribute to its effectiveness as a NoSQL database solution.

Fully Managed Service

DynamoDB is a fully managed database service, meaning that Amazon Web Services (AWS) handles all aspects of database management, including hardware provisioning, setup, configuration, scaling, and maintenance. This eliminates the operational burden on developers and allows them to focus on building applications rather than managing infrastructure.

Advantages:

- **Reduced Operational Overhead**: Developers can deploy applications without needing to worry about database maintenance, updates, or server management.

- **Automatic Updates**: DynamoDB automatically applies security patches and updates, ensuring the database is secure and up to date.

Automatic Scaling

DynamoDB features built-in automatic scaling capabilities, which allow it to dynamically adjust its read and write capacity based on application demand. This ensures that the database can handle varying workloads without manual intervention.

Advantages:

- **Seamless Performance**: During periods of high traffic, DynamoDB automatically scales to meet increased demand, preventing performance degradation.
- **Cost Efficiency**: Users can set minimum and maximum capacity thresholds, ensuring they only pay for what they use while maintaining the performance they need.

Low Latency and High Performance

DynamoDB is optimized for low-latency performance, capable of delivering single-digit millisecond response times for read and write operations. This high performance is essential for applications requiring real-time data access, such as gaming, mobile applications, and IoT systems.

Advantages:

- **Fast Data Access**: With its efficient data retrieval mechanisms, DynamoDB provides quick access to data, ensuring a responsive user experience.
- **Consistent Throughput**: DynamoDB maintains consistent performance levels even as the dataset grows, making it suitable for applications with unpredictable traffic patterns.

Global Availability and Multi-Region Support

DynamoDB offers global availability, allowing developers to create tables in multiple AWS regions. This feature enhances the availability and resilience of applications by distributing data across different geographic locations.

Advantages:

- **Disaster Recovery**: With data replicated across multiple regions, DynamoDB provides robust disaster recovery options, ensuring data durability and availability even in the event of regional outages.
- **Reduced Latency**: By hosting databases closer to end-users in different regions, applications can achieve lower latency and improved performance.

Flexible Data Model

DynamoDB supports both document and key-value data models, allowing developers to store various data types, including JSON-like documents. This flexibility makes it easier to accommodate changing data requirements without the need for extensive schema modifications.

Advantages:

- **Schema-less Design**: Developers can add or remove attributes from items without disrupting existing data, making it easier to evolve the data model as application needs change.
- **Complex Data Structures**: The ability to store nested data structures enables applications to represent complex relationships and hierarchies effectively.

Event-Driven Architecture with Streams

DynamoDB Streams provide a mechanism for capturing changes to items in a table. When items are added, updated, or deleted, DynamoDB Streams capture these events and store them in a time-ordered sequence. This feature is particularly useful for building event-driven architectures and real-time applications.

Advantages:

- **Real-Time Processing**: Developers can configure triggers that respond to changes in the database, allowing for immediate actions based on data updates. For example, an application can send notifications or trigger workflows when a new item is added.
- **Integration with AWS Lambda**: DynamoDB Streams can seamlessly integrate with AWS Lambda, enabling serverless event processing without the need for additional infrastructure.

Fine-Grained Access Control

DynamoDB offers robust security features, including fine-grained access control through AWS Identity and Access Management (IAM). This allows developers to define permissions at a granular level, specifying which users or roles can perform certain actions on tables and items.

Advantages:

- **Enhanced Security**: Fine-grained access control ensures that sensitive data is protected, allowing only authorized users to access or modify specific attributes or items.
- **Compliance**: Organizations can implement strict access controls to meet regulatory requirements and maintain data security standards.

Backup and Restore Capabilities

DynamoDB includes built-in backup and restore capabilities, allowing users to create on-demand backups of their tables. This feature is crucial for data protection and disaster recovery, ensuring that data can be restored in case of accidental deletions or corruption.

Advantages:

- **Automated Backups**: Developers can schedule automated backups, reducing the risk of data loss and simplifying the backup process.

- **Point-in-Time Recovery**: DynamoDB offers point-in-time recovery, allowing users to restore their tables to any specific moment within the last 35 days, providing an additional layer of data protection.

Integrated Security and Compliance

DynamoDB provides a range of security features, including encryption at rest and in transit, to ensure that data is protected throughout its lifecycle. These features help organizations meet compliance requirements for sensitive data management.

Advantages:

- **Data Encryption**: DynamoDB automatically encrypts data at rest using AWS Key Management Service (KMS), ensuring that sensitive data is protected against unauthorized access.
- **Compliance Standards**: DynamoDB adheres to various compliance standards, including HIPAA, PCI DSS, and GDPR, making it suitable for applications in regulated industries.

Extensive Ecosystem and Integration

DynamoDB integrates seamlessly with other AWS services, allowing developers to build comprehensive applications with minimal friction. Whether it's integrating with AWS Lambda, Amazon API Gateway, or AWS Step Functions, DynamoDB fits well within the AWS ecosystem.

Advantages:

- **Serverless Architecture**: By leveraging DynamoDB alongside other AWS services, developers can build serverless applications that automatically scale and minimize operational overhead.
- **Data Analytics**: DynamoDB can easily integrate with AWS analytics services, such as Amazon Redshift and Amazon Kinesis, enabling advanced data analysis and reporting capabilities.

Amazon DynamoDB is a powerful and versatile NoSQL database solution that excels in performance, scalability, and ease of use. Its key features—ranging from automatic scaling and low-latency access to robust security and event-driven capabilities—make it an attractive choice for a wide variety of applications. Whether you are building a web application, mobile app, or IoT solution, DynamoDB provides the tools and flexibility needed to manage data effectively.

As we continue through this book, we will explore practical examples and best practices for using DynamoDB in RESTful API development, ensuring you can leverage its capabilities to build robust and efficient applications.

Use Cases for DynamoDB in RESTful APIs

Amazon DynamoDB is particularly well-suited for developing RESTful APIs across various applications and industries. Its architecture and feature set align perfectly with the demands of modern web and mobile applications, making it a popular choice among developers. Below, we explore several use cases for DynamoDB in the context of RESTful APIs, illustrating how its capabilities enhance application performance and functionality.

E-Commerce Applications

E-commerce platforms often require real-time access to product data, user accounts, and transaction history. DynamoDB's low-latency performance and ability to scale seamlessly make it an excellent choice for building RESTful APIs in e-commerce applications.

Key Features:

- **Product Catalog Management**: Store product details, pricing, inventory levels, and descriptions in DynamoDB tables. A RESTful API can allow clients to retrieve product information quickly and efficiently.
- **User Profiles and Carts**: Manage user profiles and shopping carts by storing user data in DynamoDB. The API can facilitate operations such as adding items to the cart, retrieving saved preferences, and processing transactions.

- **Order Processing**: Handle order submissions and updates through API endpoints connected to DynamoDB, ensuring a smooth checkout experience.

Benefits:

- Fast access to product data enables quick browsing and searching, enhancing user experience.
- The ability to scale automatically during peak shopping seasons (e.g., Black Friday) ensures consistent performance without manual intervention.

Social Media Platforms

Social media applications generate vast amounts of data, including user profiles, posts, comments, and likes. DynamoDB can efficiently manage this data and provide RESTful APIs for seamless interactions among users.

Key Features:

- **User Profiles**: Store user data, including profile information, friend connections, and preferences, in a DynamoDB table. APIs can be created to manage user registration, updates, and profile retrieval.
- **Post and Comment Management**: Use DynamoDB to handle posts, comments, and reactions. The API can enable users to create, read, update, and delete posts and comments efficiently.
- **Real-Time Notifications**: Implement real-time notifications for user interactions, such as likes and comments, using DynamoDB Streams and AWS Lambda.

Benefits:

- The flexible data model allows for varying content structures (e.g., text posts, images, videos), facilitating the management of diverse user-generated content.

- Low-latency performance ensures that users receive real-time updates, improving engagement and interaction on the platform.

IoT Applications

The Internet of Things (IoT) is a rapidly growing field that generates enormous amounts of data from connected devices. DynamoDB's scalability and performance make it ideal for managing this data in RESTful APIs for IoT applications.

Key Features:

- **Device Data Management**: Store data generated by IoT devices, such as sensor readings, device statuses, and event logs, in DynamoDB. The API can provide endpoints for retrieving and processing this data.
- **Real-Time Analytics**: Leverage DynamoDB Streams to capture changes in device data and perform real-time analytics or trigger alerts based on predefined conditions.
- **Device Control**: Create RESTful APIs that allow users to send commands to IoT devices, enabling remote management and control of connected devices.

Benefits:

- The ability to handle large volumes of writes and reads from multiple devices ensures that the application can scale as more devices are added to the network.
- Real-time data processing capabilities enable immediate responses to changes in device states, enhancing user experience and functionality.

Gaming Applications

Online gaming platforms require efficient management of player profiles, game state, and leaderboards. DynamoDB's performance characteristics are well-suited for building RESTful APIs for gaming applications.

Key Features:

- **Player Profiles**: Store player account details, game statistics, and preferences in DynamoDB tables. The API can facilitate user registration, login, and profile management.
- **Game State Management**: Use DynamoDB to store and retrieve game state information, enabling players to continue their progress seamlessly across sessions.
- **Leaderboards**: Implement leaderboards by querying player statistics from DynamoDB, allowing for real-time updates and competition among players.

Benefits:

- The ability to scale automatically during high traffic periods, such as game releases or tournaments, ensures consistent performance and player satisfaction.
- Low-latency access to game state data allows for responsive gameplay, enhancing the overall gaming experience.

Content Management Systems (CMS)

Content management systems require efficient storage and retrieval of articles, multimedia, and user-generated content. DynamoDB's flexible schema and performance characteristics make it an excellent choice for CMS RESTful APIs.

Key Features:

- **Article Storage**: Store articles, blog posts, and media assets in DynamoDB. The API can allow users to create, edit, and delete content through simple endpoints.
- **User Interaction**: Manage user-generated content such as comments and ratings. The API can facilitate operations related to user feedback on published content.
- **Metadata Management**: Store metadata related to content, such as tags, categories, and author information, enabling powerful search and

filtering capabilities.

Benefits:

- The flexible data model allows for easy adaptation to changing content requirements, ensuring the CMS can evolve with user needs.
- High availability ensures that users can access and interact with content without interruptions.

Financial Services Applications

Financial services applications often require high availability, security, and real-time data processing. DynamoDB is well-suited for building RESTful APIs that manage sensitive financial data.

Key Features:

- **Transaction Management**: Store transaction records and user account information in DynamoDB. The API can facilitate secure transaction submissions, retrievals, and updates.
- **Real-Time Analytics**: Utilize DynamoDB Streams to capture transaction data and perform real-time analytics for fraud detection and reporting.
- **Account Management**: Implement account management features, allowing users to view balances, transaction histories, and account settings through the API.

Benefits:

- Strong security features, including fine-grained access control and encryption, ensure that sensitive financial data is protected.
- Low-latency performance supports real-time processing of transactions and updates, enhancing the user experience.

Health Care Applications

In the health care sector, applications must manage sensitive patient data and ensure compliance with regulations. DynamoDB offers features that support the development of RESTful APIs for health care applications.

Key Features:

- **Patient Records**: Store patient data, including medical history, treatment plans, and prescriptions, in DynamoDB. The API can provide secure access to patient information for authorized personnel.
- **Appointment Management**: Manage patient appointments and schedules through RESTful API endpoints, allowing for easy booking and updates.
- **Real-Time Health Monitoring**: Use DynamoDB to store and analyze real-time health data from connected devices (e.g., heart rate monitors), enabling timely interventions and alerts.

Benefits:

- Compliance with security and privacy regulations (e.g., HIPAA) is facilitated by DynamoDB's built-in security features.
- The ability to scale automatically ensures that the application can handle varying workloads, especially during peak periods of patient engagement.

Travel and Booking Applications

Travel and booking applications require efficient management of user preferences, itineraries, and reservations. DynamoDB's performance and scalability make it a strong candidate for building RESTful APIs in this domain.

Key Features:

- **User Profiles**: Store user profiles and preferences for travel, allowing for personalized recommendations and experiences through the API.
- **Itinerary Management**: Manage travel itineraries, including flights,

accommodations, and activities, in DynamoDB. The API can enable users to create, modify, and retrieve their itineraries.

- **Real-Time Availability**: Use DynamoDB to store real-time availability of flights, hotels, and other travel services, ensuring users receive up-to-date information.

Benefits:

- Fast access to user data and travel information enhances user experience and simplifies the booking process.
- The ability to scale during peak travel seasons ensures that the application can handle high volumes of concurrent users.

DynamoDB's capabilities make it a versatile choice for developing RESTful APIs across a wide range of applications. From e-commerce and social media to IoT and financial services, DynamoDB offers the performance, scalability, and flexibility needed to meet the demands of modern applications. As we delve deeper into this book, we will explore how to effectively implement and optimize DynamoDB in RESTful API development, ensuring your applications achieve maximum efficiency and reliability.

Setting Up DynamoDB

Setting up Amazon DynamoDB is a straightforward process that involves creating a DynamoDB table and configuring it according to your application needs. This section will guide you through the steps required to set up DynamoDB, covering everything from creating your first table to configuring settings for optimal performance.

Prerequisites

Before getting started with DynamoDB, ensure you have the following prerequisites:

- **AWS Account**: You need an active AWS account to access DynamoDB. If you don't have one, you can create a free account on the AWS website.
- **AWS Management Console**: Familiarize yourself with the AWS Management Console, which provides a web-based interface for managing AWS services, including DynamoDB.
- **AWS CLI (Optional)**: If you prefer using command-line tools, you can install and configure the AWS Command Line Interface (CLI) to interact with DynamoDB programmatically.

Accessing the DynamoDB Console

Once you have your AWS account set up, follow these steps to access the DynamoDB console:

Log in to the AWS Management Console: Go to the AWS Management Console and log in with your credentials.

Navigate to DynamoDB: In the search bar, type "DynamoDB" and select it from the results. This will take you to the DynamoDB dashboard.

Creating a DynamoDB Table

To create a new DynamoDB table, follow these steps:

Click on "Create Table": In the DynamoDB dashboard, click the "Create table" button.

Configure Table Settings:

- **Table Name**: Enter a unique name for your table. This name will be used in your API endpoints.
- **Primary Key**: Choose the primary key structure for your table:
- **Partition Key**: Specify a single attribute that will serve as the partition key. This attribute must be unique for each item.
- **Composite Key**: If you need to store multiple items with the same partition key, you can add a sort key as well. This allows for organizing related items under the same partition.

Set Up Table Options:

- **Provisioned or On-Demand Capacity**:
- **Provisioned Capacity**: Set a read and write capacity for the table. You will need to estimate the expected traffic to determine appropriate values.
- **On-Demand Capacity**: This option allows DynamoDB to automatically scale up and down based on traffic without manual intervention.
- **Auto Scaling**: If you choose provisioned capacity, you can enable auto-scaling to adjust capacity based on demand.

Configure Secondary Indexes (Optional): If you want to enable additional querying capabilities, you can set up global secondary indexes (GSIs) or local secondary indexes (LSIs). Define the partition key and sort key for each index as needed.

Set Up Stream Settings (Optional): If you want to capture changes to items in your table, you can enable DynamoDB Streams. This allows you to trigger actions in response to item modifications.

Click "Create Table": Review your settings and click the "Create table" button to finalize the setup. DynamoDB will provision the table, which may take a few moments.

Managing Your DynamoDB Table

After creating your table, you can manage it through the DynamoDB console or AWS CLI. Key management tasks include:

- **Viewing Table Details**: Click on the table name in the dashboard to view details, including item count, capacity settings, and indexes.
- **Adding Items**: You can add items to your table directly from the console. Click on the "Items" tab and select "Create item." Fill in the attribute values and save the item.
- **Querying Items**: Use the "Explore table items" option to run queries against your table. You can filter results based on attribute values and perform scans as needed.
- **Monitoring Performance**: DynamoDB provides metrics and dashboards to monitor table performance, including read and write capacity,

latency, and throttling events. This information is vital for optimizing your API performance.

Configuring IAM Permissions

To interact with DynamoDB securely, configure AWS Identity and Access Management (IAM) roles and policies. This ensures that only authorized users and applications can access your DynamoDB tables.

Create an IAM Role: In the IAM console, create a new role for your application or service that will access DynamoDB.

Attach Policies: Attach predefined policies (such as AmazonDynamoD BFullAccess) or create custom policies that grant specific permissions for actions like reading, writing, and deleting items in DynamoDB.

Apply the Role: Assign the IAM role to the AWS service or application that will interact with DynamoDB.

Accessing DynamoDB via API

After setting up your DynamoDB table and configuring IAM permissions, you can access it through RESTful APIs. There are two primary methods for interacting with DynamoDB:

- **AWS SDKs**: AWS provides SDKs for various programming languages (e.g., JavaScript, Python, Java) that simplify interactions with DynamoDB. These SDKs offer built-in methods for CRUD operations, making it easy to integrate DynamoDB into your applications.
- **HTTP API Calls**: If you prefer direct API calls, you can interact with DynamoDB using HTTP requests. You'll need to handle authentication and request formatting manually. AWS provides detailed documentation on making API calls to DynamoDB.

Best Practices for Setting Up DynamoDB

To ensure optimal performance and cost-effectiveness, consider the following best practices when setting up DynamoDB:

- **Design for Access Patterns**: Plan your data model based on expected access patterns. Consider how you will query and retrieve data when designing your tables and indexes.
- **Optimize Partition Keys**: Choose partition keys that distribute data evenly across partitions. Avoid hot keys (keys with disproportionately high access) to prevent throttling.
- **Use Global Secondary Indexes Judiciously**: While GSIs provide flexibility, they can increase costs. Create GSIs based on specific access patterns that justify their use.
- **Monitor Usage and Performance**: Regularly review your DynamoDB usage metrics and adjust capacity settings as needed. Enable Cloud-Watch alarms to notify you of any throttling events or performance issues.
- **Implement Data Expiration**: Use DynamoDB's TTL (Time to Live) feature to automatically delete items after a specified duration. This can help manage storage costs and ensure your tables remain optimized.

Setting up DynamoDB is a crucial step in leveraging its capabilities for your applications. By following the outlined steps, you can create a robust and scalable database that meets your data management needs. Understanding how to manage your DynamoDB tables and configure IAM permissions will enable you to build secure and efficient RESTful APIs that harness the power of this NoSQL database.

As we move forward in this book, we will explore how to effectively implement RESTful APIs using DynamoDB, including best practices for data modeling, querying, and optimizing performance to ensure your applications deliver exceptional user experiences.

Introuction to PostgreSQL

O verview of PostgreSQL
    PostgreSQL is a powerful, open-source relational database management system (RDBMS) known for its robustness, extensibility, and adherence to SQL standards. It is designed to handle a wide range of workloads, from small single-machine applications to large-scale data warehousing and web applications. This section provides a comprehensive overview of PostgreSQL, covering its architecture, key features, advantages, and typical use cases.

Understanding PostgreSQL

PostgreSQL was developed in the late 1980s as part of the POSTGRES project at the University of California, Berkeley. It has since evolved into a mature database system that is widely used across various industries. The key characteristics of PostgreSQL include:

- **Relational Database Management System**: PostgreSQL is fundamentally a relational database, meaning it stores data in structured tables with predefined schemas. Relationships between tables are established through foreign keys, allowing for complex queries and data integrity.
- **ACID Compliance**: PostgreSQL adheres to the ACID (Atomicity, Consistency, Isolation, Durability) properties, ensuring reliable transactions and data integrity. This makes it suitable for applications where data consistency is critical, such as financial systems.
- **Extensibility**: One of PostgreSQL's standout features is its extensibility. Users can define custom data types, operators, and functions, enabling

PostgreSQL to accommodate a wide variety of data and application needs. Additionally, users can create extensions that enhance PostgreSQL's functionality, such as PostGIS for geospatial data.

Key Features of PostgreSQL

PostgreSQL offers a rich set of features that make it a compelling choice for developers and organizations:

- **SQL Compliance**: PostgreSQL follows the SQL standard closely, supporting a wide range of SQL features, including complex joins, subqueries, window functions, and Common Table Expressions (CTEs). This compliance facilitates a smooth transition for users coming from other SQL databases.
- **Support for JSON and NoSQL Features**: PostgreSQL has robust support for storing and querying JSON data. This allows developers to leverage both relational and NoSQL paradigms within the same database, making it suitable for applications that require flexibility in data storage.
- **Full-Text Search**: PostgreSQL provides built-in full-text search capabilities, allowing users to perform complex search queries across large datasets. This feature is useful for applications that require searching through large volumes of text data, such as content management systems and e-commerce platforms.
- **Concurrency Control**: PostgreSQL uses Multi-Version Concurrency Control (MVCC) to handle concurrent transactions efficiently. MVCC ensures that readers do not block writers and vice versa, allowing for high levels of concurrency without sacrificing performance.
- **Replication and High Availability**: PostgreSQL supports various replication methods, including streaming replication and logical replication, enabling high availability and disaster recovery setups. These features are essential for mission-critical applications that require continuous uptime.
- **Partitioning**: PostgreSQL allows for table partitioning, which enables

large tables to be divided into smaller, more manageable pieces. This can enhance query performance and improve data management by reducing the amount of data scanned during operations.

- **Advanced Indexing Options**: PostgreSQL supports a variety of indexing techniques, including B-trees, hash indexes, GiST, GIN, and BRIN indexes. These indexing options enhance query performance and allow for optimized data retrieval based on different use cases.

Advantages of PostgreSQL

PostgreSQL has several advantages that contribute to its popularity among developers and organizations:

- **Open Source**: Being an open-source project, PostgreSQL is free to use and distribute. Its community-driven development ensures continuous improvements, bug fixes, and feature enhancements, making it a reliable choice for organizations of all sizes.
- **Cross-Platform Compatibility**: PostgreSQL is compatible with various operating systems, including Linux, Windows, and macOS. This flexibility allows organizations to deploy PostgreSQL in different environments based on their requirements.
- **Strong Community Support**: PostgreSQL boasts a vibrant and active community that contributes to its development and offers extensive documentation, tutorials, and forums for troubleshooting. This support network is invaluable for developers seeking assistance or learning resources.
- **Robust Security Features**: PostgreSQL includes advanced security features such as role-based access control, SSL encryption for data in transit, and data encryption at rest. These features make it suitable for applications that handle sensitive information.
- **Integration with Other Technologies**: PostgreSQL easily integrates with a variety of programming languages, frameworks, and tools, such as Python, Java, Node.js, and web development frameworks like Django and Ruby on Rails. This integration capability enhances its versatility

for different application development needs.

Typical Use Cases for PostgreSQL

PostgreSQL is well-suited for a variety of applications across different industries. Here are some common use cases:

- **Web Applications**: Many web applications use PostgreSQL to manage user data, content, and transactions. Its ability to handle high concurrency makes it ideal for dynamic websites and applications that require real-time interactions.
- **Data Warehousing and Analytics**: PostgreSQL's support for large datasets, complex queries, and advanced analytics functions allows organizations to use it as a data warehouse solution. Businesses can perform analytical queries on historical data to gain insights and drive decision-making.
- **Geospatial Applications**: With the PostGIS extension, PostgreSQL can handle geospatial data and perform geographic calculations. This makes it suitable for applications such as mapping services, location-based analytics, and urban planning.
- **Financial Services**: PostgreSQL's ACID compliance and robust transaction support make it a preferred choice for financial applications, including banking systems, payment gateways, and trading platforms.
- **Content Management Systems (CMS)**: Many content management systems utilize PostgreSQL to store and manage articles, multimedia, and user-generated content. Its extensibility allows for customized content types and workflows.

PostgreSQL Architecture

Understanding the architecture of PostgreSQL is key to leveraging its capabilities effectively. The architecture can be divided into several components:

- **Postmaster**: The postmaster is the main server process responsible for managing the database system. It handles client connections, forks new backend processes, and manages system resources.

- **Backend Processes**: When a client connects to PostgreSQL, the postmaster forks a new backend process to handle the client's requests. Each backend process is responsible for executing SQL commands, managing transactions, and interacting with the database.
- **Shared Buffers**: PostgreSQL uses a shared memory area called shared buffers to cache data pages. This caching mechanism improves performance by reducing disk I/O operations.
- **WAL (Write-Ahead Logging)**: PostgreSQL employs a write-ahead logging mechanism to ensure data durability. Changes are first recorded in the WAL before being written to the database, allowing for recovery in case of failures.
- **Storage Manager**: The storage manager is responsible for managing the physical storage of data, including tables, indexes, and WAL files. It handles the organization of data on disk and ensures efficient data retrieval.

PostgreSQL is a powerful and versatile relational database management system that combines robust features, performance, and extensibility. Its support for advanced data types, full-text search, and complex queries makes it suitable for a wide range of applications, from web and mobile apps to data analytics and geospatial solutions. As we progress through this book, we will explore how to effectively use PostgreSQL in conjunction with RESTful API development, focusing on practical examples, best practices, and optimization techniques to maximize the efficiency and reliability of your applications.

Key Features and Advantages of PostgreSQL

PostgreSQL is celebrated for its rich feature set and robust performance, making it a top choice for developers and organizations alike. Understanding these features and advantages can help you leverage PostgreSQL effectively in your applications. This section highlights the key features and benefits that distinguish PostgreSQL from other database management systems.

Advanced SQL Compliance

PostgreSQL is renowned for its strong adherence to SQL standards, which makes it easier for developers familiar with SQL to work with it. This compliance includes support for various SQL features such as:

- **Complex Queries**: PostgreSQL allows for intricate queries involving joins, subqueries, and aggregations. Its support for Common Table Expressions (CTEs) simplifies complex query logic and improves readability.
- **Window Functions**: These functions enable calculations across a set of rows related to the current row, which is particularly useful for analytics and reporting.
- **Custom Functions**: PostgreSQL allows users to create custom functions and procedures in various programming languages (e.g., PL/pgSQL, PL/Python), extending its capabilities beyond standard SQL.

Extensibility

One of PostgreSQL's standout features is its extensibility. Users can customize the database by adding new data types, operators, and index methods. This flexibility is advantageous for applications with specific data management needs.

- **Custom Data Types**: Developers can define custom data types tailored to their applications, allowing for more efficient data storage and processing.
- **Extensions**: PostgreSQL supports a wide range of extensions that enhance its functionality, such as PostGIS for geospatial data, hstore for key-value pairs, and full-text search capabilities.

- **Foreign Data Wrappers (FDWs)**: FDWs enable PostgreSQL to connect to external data sources, such as other databases or APIs, allowing for seamless integration of heterogeneous data.

Robust Concurrency Control

PostgreSQL utilizes Multi-Version Concurrency Control (MVCC) to manage concurrent transactions effectively. This approach allows multiple transactions to occur simultaneously without blocking each other, enhancing performance and user experience.

- **Non-Blocking Reads**: With MVCC, readers do not block writers and vice versa. This enables high levels of concurrency, making PostgreSQL suitable for applications with many simultaneous users.
- **Transaction Isolation Levels**: PostgreSQL supports various transaction isolation levels, allowing developers to choose the appropriate level of consistency for their applications. This flexibility helps balance performance and data integrity.

High Availability and Replication

PostgreSQL provides several options for ensuring high availability and data durability, making it suitable for mission-critical applications.

- **Streaming Replication**: PostgreSQL supports streaming replication, which allows for real-time data replication to standby servers. This setup enables failover capabilities, ensuring continued availability in case of primary server failure.
- **Logical Replication**: Logical replication allows selective replication of specific tables or rows, making it useful for scenarios where only a subset of data needs to be shared across servers.
- **Automatic Failover**: Tools like Patroni and repmgr facilitate automatic failover, allowing applications to switch to standby servers without manual intervention during primary server outages.

Advanced Indexing Options

PostgreSQL offers a wide variety of indexing methods that optimize data retrieval and improve query performance. This includes:

- **B-Tree Indexes**: The default index type that provides fast access to data for equality and range queries.
- **GIN and GiST Indexes**: Generalized Inverted Index (GIN) and Generalized Search Tree (GiST) indexes support complex data types like arrays, JSONB, and geometric data, enhancing search capabilities.
- **BRIN Indexes**: Block Range INdexes (BRIN) are efficient for large datasets, allowing PostgreSQL to store summary information about the data blocks, leading to reduced storage requirements and improved performance.

JSON Support

PostgreSQL provides robust support for JSON data types, allowing developers to store and manipulate semi-structured data alongside traditional relational data. This feature makes PostgreSQL a strong candidate for applications that require flexibility in data representation.

- **JSON and JSONB Types**: PostgreSQL supports both JSON and JSONB (binary JSON) data types. JSONB provides advantages in terms of storage efficiency and performance for queries, as it is stored in a binary format that enables indexing.
- **Powerful JSON Functions**: PostgreSQL includes numerous built-in functions for querying and manipulating JSON data, making it easy to work with complex data structures directly within the database.

Full-Text Search Capabilities

PostgreSQL includes powerful full-text search capabilities, allowing for efficient searching of textual data. This feature is particularly useful for applications that require searching through large volumes of text.

- **Text Search Data Type**: PostgreSQL has a dedicated data type for text search, enabling the indexing of documents for fast retrieval based on search terms.
- **Customizable Search**: Users can define custom dictionaries and configurations for different languages, enhancing the search experience for international applications.
- **Ranking and Highlighting**: PostgreSQL provides functions to rank search results based on relevance and highlight search terms within the retrieved documents.

Strong Security Features

PostgreSQL is equipped with robust security features that help protect sensitive data and ensure compliance with various regulations.

- **Role-Based Access Control**: PostgreSQL supports fine-grained access control through roles and permissions, allowing administrators to define which users can access specific data and perform certain actions.
- **SSL Encryption**: PostgreSQL supports SSL encryption for data in transit, ensuring that sensitive information remains secure during transmission over networks.
- **Data Encryption at Rest**: PostgreSQL allows for data encryption at rest, protecting stored data from unauthorized access. This is essential for applications dealing with sensitive or regulated information.

Comprehensive Backup and Restore Options

PostgreSQL offers various options for backing up and restoring data, ensuring data durability and protection against loss.

- **Physical Backups**: Use tools like pg_basebackup for creating physical backups of the database, allowing for point-in-time recovery.
- **Logical Backups**: Logical backups can be created using the pg_dump utility, which allows for selective backup of specific tables or schemas.
- **Point-in-Time Recovery**: PostgreSQL supports point-in-time recov-

ery (PITR), enabling users to restore the database to a specific state using WAL files, ensuring minimal data loss in the event of a failure.

Extensive Ecosystem and Community Support

PostgreSQL is backed by a vibrant community and a rich ecosystem of tools, libraries, and frameworks.

- **Active Community**: The PostgreSQL community is active in development and support, providing extensive documentation, tutorials, and forums for troubleshooting.
- **Third-Party Tools**: A wide array of third-party tools and extensions enhance PostgreSQL's capabilities, including monitoring tools (e.g., pgAdmin, Datadog), management tools (e.g., pgAdmin, DBeaver), and performance optimization tools.
- **Integration with Other Technologies**: PostgreSQL easily integrates with various programming languages and frameworks, such as Python, Java, and Node.js, making it a flexible choice for diverse application development.

PostgreSQL is a powerful and feature-rich relational database management system that excels in performance, extensibility, and compliance. Its advanced SQL support, flexible data handling capabilities, and robust security features make it suitable for a wide range of applications, from web and mobile apps to data analytics and geospatial solutions. As we move forward in this book, we will explore how to effectively implement PostgreSQL in conjunction with RESTful API development, focusing on practical examples, best practices, and optimization techniques to ensure your applications achieve maximum efficiency and reliability.

Use Cases for PostgreSQL in RESTful APIs

PostgreSQL's robust feature set, compliance with SQL standards, and extensibility make it an excellent choice for developing RESTful APIs across a variety of applications and industries. Below, we explore several use cases for PostgreSQL in the context of RESTful APIs, illustrating how its capabilities enhance application performance, scalability, and flexibility.

Content Management Systems (CMS)

PostgreSQL is a popular choice for powering content management systems due to its ability to handle complex queries, relationships, and diverse data types.

Key Features:

- **Structured Data Storage**: CMS applications often require storing a variety of content types, including articles, images, and metadata. PostgreSQL's relational structure allows for efficient organization and retrieval of this data.
- **Full-Text Search**: PostgreSQL's full-text search capabilities enable users to search through large volumes of text quickly and efficiently, enhancing content discovery.

Benefits:

- The ability to define relationships between content types (e.g., authors, categories) supports rich querying capabilities, allowing users to filter and sort content based on various criteria.
- Customizable workflows and permissions can be implemented easily using PostgreSQL's role-based access control, ensuring that content is managed securely.

E-Commerce Platforms

E-commerce applications require reliable data storage for products, user profiles, transactions, and inventory management. PostgreSQL provides the necessary features to build robust RESTful APIs that handle these requirements.

Key Features:

- **Data Integrity**: With ACID compliance, PostgreSQL ensures that transactions, such as order placements and payment processing, are completed accurately and reliably.
- **Complex Relationships**: The relational model allows for easy management of complex relationships, such as products, categories, and customer orders.

Benefits:

- PostgreSQL's ability to handle large datasets and high concurrency makes it suitable for high-traffic e-commerce websites, especially during peak seasons.
- Advanced indexing options, such as GIN and GiST, enable fast searching and filtering of products, improving user experience.

Financial Applications

Financial services applications demand high levels of data integrity, security, and performance. PostgreSQL is well-equipped to meet these requirements, making it a preferred choice for building RESTful APIs in this domain.

Key Features:

- **Transaction Management**: PostgreSQL's robust transaction support ensures that financial transactions are processed reliably, with rollback capabilities in case of errors.
- **Strong Security Features**: Role-based access control, SSL encryption, and data encryption at rest protect sensitive financial data.

Benefits:

- The ability to run complex analytical queries on transaction data allows financial institutions to gain insights and make informed decisions.
- PostgreSQL's support for JSON and non-relational features allows for

flexible storage of diverse financial data types, enhancing application development.

Social Media Applications

Social media platforms generate vast amounts of user-generated content and require efficient management of user interactions. PostgreSQL's scalability and query capabilities make it suitable for developing RESTful APIs for these applications.

Key Features:

- **User Profile Management**: PostgreSQL can efficiently store and manage user profiles, connections, and preferences, facilitating easy access and updates via the API.
- **Post and Comment Storage**: The relational model allows for organized storage of posts, comments, likes, and shares, with efficient querying for user feeds.

Benefits:

- The ability to perform real-time analytics on user interactions supports features like trending topics and personalized content recommendations.
- PostgreSQL's full-text search capabilities enable users to search for posts and content easily, enhancing engagement on the platform.

Geospatial Applications

With the PostGIS extension, PostgreSQL becomes a powerful platform for managing and querying geospatial data. This makes it a strong candidate for RESTful APIs in geospatial applications.

Key Features:

- **Geospatial Data Types**: PostGIS provides specialized data types for handling geographic information, enabling complex spatial queries and analysis.

- **Spatial Indexing**: Efficient spatial indexing enhances the performance of location-based queries, making it easier to retrieve relevant data.

Benefits:

- Applications such as mapping services, urban planning tools, and location-based analytics can leverage PostgreSQL's capabilities to manage and visualize geospatial data effectively.
- The ability to integrate geospatial queries into a RESTful API allows for powerful features, such as finding nearby locations or analyzing spatial relationships.

Data Analytics and Business Intelligence

PostgreSQL is increasingly used for data analytics and business intelligence applications due to its robust querying capabilities and support for complex data types.

Key Features:

- **Complex Analytical Queries**: PostgreSQL supports advanced SQL features, such as window functions and Common Table Expressions (CTEs), which are essential for analytical queries.
- **Integration with BI Tools**: PostgreSQL can easily integrate with various business intelligence and data visualization tools, enabling organizations to analyze and visualize their data effectively.

Benefits:

- Organizations can build RESTful APIs that provide access to analytical data, allowing internal tools or third-party applications to consume insights in real-time.
- The ability to handle large datasets efficiently makes PostgreSQL suitable for data warehousing solutions.

Health Care Applications

In the health care sector, applications must manage sensitive patient data while ensuring compliance with regulations. PostgreSQL offers features that support the development of secure and efficient RESTful APIs for health care applications.

Key Features:

- **Data Security**: PostgreSQL's robust security features, including encryption and access control, help protect sensitive patient information.
- **ACID Compliance**: The reliability of transactions ensures that patient records and appointment scheduling are managed accurately.

Benefits:

- The ability to store and query complex data structures allows health care applications to manage diverse patient data effectively, including medical histories and treatment plans.
- Integration with health monitoring devices can be facilitated through RESTful APIs that query and store real-time patient data.

Internet of Things (IoT) Applications

IoT applications generate significant amounts of data from connected devices. PostgreSQL's scalability and data handling capabilities make it suitable for managing this data in RESTful APIs.

Key Features:

- **Time-Series Data Handling**: PostgreSQL can efficiently manage time-series data, which is crucial for applications that monitor IoT devices over time.
- **JSON Support**: The ability to store and query JSON data allows for flexible storage of device data, enabling easier integration with diverse IoT devices.

Benefits:

- The capacity to scale and handle high write volumes ensures that applications can effectively manage data from numerous connected devices.
- Real-time analytics on device data can be performed through RESTful APIs, enabling timely insights and actions based on device performance.

PostgreSQL's capabilities make it an excellent choice for developing RESTful APIs across various applications. From content management systems and e-commerce platforms to financial services and IoT applications, PostgreSQL provides the performance, scalability, and flexibility needed to meet diverse data management requirements. As we move forward in this book, we will explore how to effectively implement and optimize PostgreSQL in RESTful API development, ensuring that your applications deliver exceptional performance and reliability.

Setting Up PostgreSQL

Setting up PostgreSQL is a straightforward process that involves installing the database, configuring it for your needs, and creating the necessary databases and tables for your applications. This section will guide you through the steps to set up PostgreSQL, from installation to initial configuration and management.

Prerequisites

Before you begin the installation of PostgreSQL, ensure you have the following prerequisites:

- **Operating System**: PostgreSQL is compatible with various operating systems, including Windows, macOS, and several Linux distributions (such as Ubuntu, CentOS, and Debian). Make sure your system meets the necessary requirements for installation.

- **Sufficient Permissions**: You will need administrative or root access to install PostgreSQL on your machine.
- **Internet Connection**: An internet connection may be required to download installation packages and dependencies.

Installing PostgreSQL

The installation process varies depending on the operating system you are using. Below are the steps for installing PostgreSQL on common platforms:

Installation on Windows

Download the Installer: Visit the PostgreSQL official website and download the installer for Windows.

Run the Installer: Double-click the downloaded installer. Follow the on-screen instructions to select the installation directory and components to install.

Set the Password: During the installation, you will be prompted to set a password for the default PostgreSQL superuser account (typically named "postgres"). Make sure to remember this password, as you will need it to access the database.

Select Port Number: The default port for PostgreSQL is 5432. You can accept this default or change it if necessary.

Complete Installation: Finish the installation process, and the PostgreSQL service will start automatically.

Verify Installation: Open the command prompt and run the following command to check the installed version:

```
psql --version
```

Installation on macOS

Use Homebrew: If you have Homebrew installed, you can easily install PostgreSQL using the following command in the terminal:

```
brew install postgresql
```

1. **Initialize Database**: After installation, initialize the PostgreSQL database using:

```
brew services start postgresql
```

1. **Verify Installation**: Check the installed version with:

```
psql --version
```

Start PostgreSQL: If not already running, you can start PostgreSQL with:

```
pg_ctl -D /usr/local/var/postgres start
```

Installation on Linux (Ubuntu)

1. **Update Package List**: Open the terminal and update your package list:

```
sudo apt update
```

1. **Install PostgreSQL**: Install PostgreSQL with the following command:

```
sudo apt install postgresql postgresql-contrib
```

Start PostgreSQL Service: After installation, the PostgreSQL service should start automatically. You can check its status with:

```
sudo systemctl status postgresql
```

Verify Installation: Use the following command to verify the installed version:

```
psql --version
```

Initial Configuration

After installation, you may want to perform some initial configuration tasks to tailor PostgreSQL to your needs.

Accessing PostgreSQL

By default, PostgreSQL creates a superuser named "postgres." You can access the PostgreSQL command-line interface (psql) by switching to the postgres user or by running psql as an admin user:

- **Switch User** (Linux/macOS):

```
sudo -i -u postgres
psql
```

- **Directly Run psql** (Windows):

```
psql -U postgres
```

Creating a New Database

Once inside the PostgreSQL prompt, you can create a new database using the following command:

```
CREATE DATABASE my_database;
```

Replace my_database with your desired database name.

Creating a New User

You can create a new user with specific privileges using the following commands:

```
CREATE USER my_user WITH PASSWORD 'my_password';
GRANT ALL PRIVILEGES ON DATABASE my_database TO my_user;
```

Replace my_user and my_password with your desired username and password.

Configuring Authentication

PostgreSQL uses a configuration file named pg_hba.conf to manage client authentication. You may need to edit this file to specify how users can connect to the database:

- **Locate the Configuration File**: The file is usually found in the PostgreSQL data directory (e.g., /etc/postgresql/12/main/pg_hba.conf for Ubuntu).
- **Edit the File**: Use a text editor to open the file and modify the

authentication method. For example, to allow local connections with password authentication, you might have lines like:

```
# TYPE  DATABASE      USER          ADDRESS
METHOD
local   all           all
md5
```

- **Restart PostgreSQL**: After making changes, restart the PostgreSQL service for the changes to take effect:

```
sudo systemctl restart postgresql
```

Managing PostgreSQL

Once PostgreSQL is set up, you can manage your database using the following methods:

Using the psql Command-Line Interface

The psql command-line tool allows you to execute SQL commands directly. Here are some common commands:

- **List Databases**:

```
\l
```

- **Connect to a Database**:

```
\c my_database
```

- **List Tables**:

```
\dt
```

- **Run a Query**:

```
SELECT * FROM my_table;
```

Using PostgreSQL GUI Tools

Several graphical user interface (GUI) tools are available for managing PostgreSQL databases, which can simplify database management:

- **pgAdmin**: A popular open-source GUI tool for managing PostgreSQL databases. It provides a web-based interface for executing queries, managing databases, and visualizing data.
- **DBeaver**: A universal database management tool that supports multiple databases, including PostgreSQL. It offers a rich user interface and features for managing database connections and running queries.

Backup and Restore

PostgreSQL provides robust options for backing up and restoring databases, ensuring data durability and protection against loss.

Backing Up a Database

You can create a backup of your database using the pg_dump utility. For example:

```
pg_dump my_database > my_database_backup.sql
```

This command creates a text file containing SQL commands to recreate the database.

5.2 Restoring a Database

To restore a database from a backup file, you can use the psql command:

```
psql my_database < my_database_backup.sql
```

Performance Tuning

To ensure optimal performance of your PostgreSQL database, consider the following tuning practices:

- **Memory Configuration**: Adjust the shared_buffers parameter in the postgresql.conf file to allocate more memory for caching database pages. A common starting point is 25% of system RAM.
- **Connection Pooling**: Use a connection pooler (like PgBouncer) to manage database connections efficiently, especially for applications with high concurrency.
- **Query Optimization**: Regularly analyze your queries using EXPLAIN to understand their execution plans. Optimize indexes and queries based on usage patterns.

Setting up PostgreSQL is a crucial step in leveraging its capabilities for your applications. By following the outlined steps, you can create a robust, secure, and scalable database that meets your data management needs. Understanding how to manage your PostgreSQL instance, configure users and permissions, and perform backups will enable you to build secure and efficient RESTful APIs that harness the power of this relational database.

As we progress through this book, we will explore how to effectively implement RESTful APIs using PostgreSQL, focusing on practical examples, best practices, and optimization techniques to ensure your applications deliver exceptional performance and reliability.

Comparing DynamoDB and PostgreSQL

Data Models – Key-Value vs. Relational

When selecting a database system for your application, understanding the underlying data models is critical. The choice between a key-value data model, like that used by DynamoDB, and a relational data model, such as that employed by PostgreSQL, has significant implications for how data is structured, accessed, and managed. This section will explore the fundamental differences between key-value and relational data models, highlighting the strengths and weaknesses of each approach.

Key-Value Data Model

The key-value data model is one of the simplest types of data models, where each piece of data (a value) is associated with a unique key. This model is highly flexible and allows for rapid access to data based on its key, making it ideal for specific use cases.

Structure of Key-Value Stores

In a key-value store, data is organized as a collection of key-value pairs:

- **Key**: A unique identifier used to retrieve the corresponding value. Keys are usually strings, but they can be of various types depending on the implementation.
- **Value**: The data associated with the key. Values can be simple data types (like strings or numbers) or complex data structures (like JSON objects or binary data).

Example: In DynamoDB, a simple key-value pair might look like this:

Key	Value
user:1001	{ "name": "John", "age": 30 }
user:1002	{ "name": "Jane", "age": 25 }

Advantages of Key-Value Data Models

- **Simplicity**: The key-value model is straightforward and easy to understand. Developers can quickly retrieve or update data using the key without needing to understand complex relationships.
- **Performance**: Key-value stores are optimized for high-speed retrieval of data based on keys. This makes them suitable for applications that require low-latency access to specific pieces of data, such as caching layers or session management.
- **Scalability**: Key-value databases, like DynamoDB, can scale horizontally by distributing data across multiple servers. This architecture allows them to handle large volumes of data and high transaction loads.
- **Flexibility**: The schema-less nature of key-value stores means that data can evolve without requiring migrations or complex schema changes. Developers can add or remove fields from the value without impacting existing data.

Limitations of Key-Value Data Models

- **Limited Query Capabilities**: While key-value stores excel at retrieving data by key, they often lack the sophisticated querying capabilities found in relational databases. Complex queries involving multiple keys or conditions may require additional logic in the application layer.
- **No Relationships**: Key-value databases do not natively support relationships between data entities. Developers must implement their own mechanisms for managing relationships, which can lead to increased complexity in data management.
- **Data Redundancy**: In a key-value model, it's common to duplicate

data across different keys to facilitate quick access. This redundancy can lead to increased storage costs and maintenance challenges.

Relational Data Model

The relational data model organizes data into structured tables with predefined schemas. Each table consists of rows and columns, where rows represent individual records and columns represent attributes of those records.

Structure of Relational Databases

In a relational database, data is stored in tables that can be related to each other through foreign keys:

- **Tables**: Each table represents an entity (e.g., users, products, orders). Tables have a defined schema, which specifies the data types and constraints for each column.
- **Rows**: Each row in a table represents a single record. For example, in a "Users" table, each row would contain information about a different user.
- **Columns**: Each column in a table corresponds to a specific attribute of the entity. For example, the "Users" table might have columns for user_id, name, email, and age.

user_id	name	email	age
1	John	john@example.com	30
2	Jane	jane@example.com	25

Advantages of Relational Data Models

- **Complex Queries**: Relational databases support complex queries using SQL, enabling developers to retrieve and manipulate data across multiple tables. This allows for sophisticated reporting and data analysis.

- **Data Integrity**: Relational databases enforce data integrity through constraints (e.g., primary keys, foreign keys, unique constraints). This ensures that relationships between data entities are maintained and that invalid data cannot be entered.
- **Relationships**: The relational model inherently supports relationships between tables, allowing developers to define one-to-one, one-to-many, and many-to-many relationships. This makes it easy to navigate related data.
- **Normalization**: Data can be normalized to minimize redundancy and improve data integrity. This means that the same piece of information is stored only once, reducing the risk of inconsistency.

Limitations of Relational Data Models

- **Complexity**: The structured nature of relational databases can introduce complexity, particularly when dealing with many tables and relationships. Developers must design schemas carefully and manage relationships explicitly.
- **Scalability Challenges**: Traditional relational databases may struggle to scale horizontally compared to key-value stores. While modern relational databases offer sharding and clustering options, these solutions can add complexity to deployment and maintenance.
- **Rigid Schema**: Changes to the database schema (e.g., adding new columns or changing data types) can be cumbersome and may require downtime or complex migration processes.

Use Cases for Key-Value vs. Relational Models

Choosing between a key-value model and a relational model often depends on the specific requirements of the application:

When to Use Key-Value Stores (DynamoDB)

- **Real-Time Applications**: Key-value stores excel in scenarios where rapid data access is critical, such as caching, session management, or user preferences.
- **High-Volume Data**: Applications that generate vast amounts of data, such as IoT devices or logging systems, can benefit from the scalability and performance of key-value stores.
- **Flexible Data Structures**: If your application requires storing unstructured or semi-structured data, key-value stores provide the flexibility to accommodate evolving data models.

When to Use Relational Databases (PostgreSQL)

- **Complex Relationships**: Applications that require managing complex relationships between entities, such as e-commerce platforms or content management systems, are better suited for relational databases.
- **Data Integrity and Consistency**: If your application demands strong data integrity and consistency, relational databases provide the mechanisms to enforce these requirements through constraints and transactions.
- **Advanced Analytics**: Applications that require complex queries, reporting, and analytics benefit from the powerful SQL capabilities of relational databases.

The choice between a key-value data model and a relational data model is critical and should be based on the specific needs of your application. Key-value stores, like DynamoDB, offer simplicity, flexibility, and performance for high-volume, real-time data access, while relational databases, like PostgreSQL, excel in handling complex queries, relationships, and data integrity.

As we continue through this book, we will explore how to effectively leverage both DynamoDB and PostgreSQL in RESTful API development, ensuring you can select the appropriate data model for your application's requirements and maximize its performance and reliability.

Performance Considerations: DynamoDB vs. PostgreSQL

When developing applications that rely on database systems, understanding performance considerations is critical to ensure efficient operation and a positive user experience. Both DynamoDB and PostgreSQL have unique performance characteristics, strengths, and trade-offs. This section explores key performance considerations for each database system, including scalability, query performance, latency, and overall system design.

Scalability

DynamoDB:

- **Automatic Scaling**: DynamoDB offers built-in automatic scaling, which adjusts read and write capacity based on traffic demands. This feature allows applications to handle unpredictable workloads without manual intervention.
- **Horizontal Scalability**: As a distributed database, DynamoDB can seamlessly scale horizontally by adding additional nodes. This allows it to accommodate significant increases in data volume and user traffic.
- **Partition Management**: DynamoDB automatically manages partitions to distribute data and workload evenly across the system, which optimizes performance as the dataset grows.

PostgreSQL:

- **Vertical Scaling**: PostgreSQL typically scales vertically by upgrading hardware resources (CPU, RAM, SSD). While this can effectively handle increased loads, there are limits to vertical scaling, and hardware costs can be significant.
- **Horizontal Scaling Options**: PostgreSQL supports various techniques for horizontal scaling, such as table partitioning, sharding, and logical replication. However, these methods often require additional configuration and management effort.
- **Read Replicas**: PostgreSQL allows the creation of read replicas to distribute read traffic, which can help improve performance for read-

heavy workloads.

Query Performance
DynamoDB:

- **Optimized for Key-Based Access**: DynamoDB is highly optimized for accessing data via primary keys, resulting in very low latency for read and write operations. However, its performance may degrade when performing complex queries that require filtering or sorting by non-key attributes.
- **Indexing**: The use of Global Secondary Indexes (GSIs) and Local Secondary Indexes (LSIs) can improve query performance by allowing queries on non-key attributes. However, excessive reliance on indexes can lead to increased storage costs and may affect write performance due to the need to update multiple indexes.

PostgreSQL:

- **Complex Query Optimization**: PostgreSQL is designed to handle complex queries efficiently, leveraging its advanced query planner and optimizer. It can execute intricate SQL queries, including those with joins, subqueries, and aggregations, with optimized performance.
- **Advanced Indexing Options**: PostgreSQL supports various indexing techniques (B-tree, GIN, GiST, BRIN), which can significantly enhance query performance. Developers can choose the most suitable indexing method based on their query patterns and data types.
- **Materialized Views**: PostgreSQL allows the creation of materialized views, which store the results of a query for faster access. This can improve performance for frequently accessed complex queries.

Latency
DynamoDB:

- **Single-Digit Millisecond Response Times**: DynamoDB is designed for low-latency access, often delivering single-digit millisecond response times for reads and writes. This performance is critical for applications requiring real-time interactions, such as gaming or IoT systems.
- **Consistent Performance**: DynamoDB maintains consistent performance regardless of the data size or number of requests, making it suitable for high-traffic applications.

PostgreSQL:

- **Variable Latency**: PostgreSQL can deliver low latency for simple queries, but latency may increase with complex queries involving multiple joins, aggregations, or large datasets. Performance tuning and query optimization are essential to minimize latency.
- **Connection Overhead**: Establishing connections to PostgreSQL can introduce latency, especially in high-concurrency scenarios. Connection pooling can mitigate this by reusing connections, reducing overhead for each request.

Data Retrieval Patterns
DynamoDB:

- **Optimized for Primary Key Access**: DynamoDB excels when data is retrieved using primary keys. Its performance diminishes for queries that require scanning large datasets or accessing items by non-key attributes.
- **Batch Operations**: DynamoDB supports batch read and write operations, allowing multiple items to be retrieved or modified in a single API call. This can improve performance in scenarios where multiple operations need to be executed together.

PostgreSQL:

- **Rich Querying Capabilities**: PostgreSQL supports complex queries with filtering, sorting, and aggregation, making it suitable for applications requiring diverse data retrieval patterns.
- **Join Operations**: PostgreSQL is optimized for performing join operations across multiple tables. This capability is crucial for applications with interconnected data entities.

Transaction Management
DynamoDB:

- **Limited Transaction Support**: While DynamoDB supports transactions, they are limited compared to traditional relational databases. Transactions in DynamoDB can involve up to 25 items or 4 MB of data, which may be restrictive for some applications.
- **Eventual Consistency**: By default, reads from DynamoDB are eventually consistent, which may introduce temporary discrepancies in data retrieval. However, strongly consistent reads can be configured at the cost of increased latency.

PostgreSQL:

- **ACID Transactions**: PostgreSQL offers full ACID compliance, ensuring that transactions are reliable and consistent. This is essential for applications where data integrity is paramount, such as financial systems.
- **Savepoints**: PostgreSQL supports savepoints, allowing developers to set intermediate points within a transaction. This enables partial rollbacks and enhances error handling within complex transaction workflows.

Cost Considerations
DynamoDB:

- **Pay-as-You-Go Pricing**: DynamoDB's pricing model is based on the provisioned capacity (read/write units) and storage used. This model can be cost-effective for applications with variable workloads but may become expensive with high constant usage.
- **Cost Control**: Users can set limits on maximum capacity and use on-demand capacity for unpredictable workloads to manage costs effectively.

PostgreSQL:

- **License-Free**: As an open-source database, PostgreSQL itself does not incur licensing fees. However, costs may arise from infrastructure (servers, storage) and maintenance.
- **Resource Utilization**: The cost associated with PostgreSQL is largely tied to the underlying hardware and resources used. Proper optimization and scaling strategies can help control these costs.

When considering performance, both DynamoDB and PostgreSQL offer distinct advantages depending on the specific needs of your application. DynamoDB excels in scenarios requiring low-latency access, scalability, and flexibility in data structure, making it ideal for key-value access patterns and real-time applications. Conversely, PostgreSQL shines in complex querying, data integrity, and relational management, making it suitable for applications with intricate relationships and reporting needs.

Understanding these performance considerations is crucial for selecting the appropriate database solution for your RESTful API development. As we continue through this book, we will explore how to effectively implement and optimize both DynamoDB and PostgreSQL in your applications, ensuring that you can leverage their strengths to deliver exceptional performance and reliability.

Scalability and Cost: Comparing DynamoDB and PostgreSQL

Scalability and cost are two critical factors to consider when selecting a database solution for your applications. Understanding how each database system handles scalability and the associated costs can help you make informed decisions that align with your project requirements and budget constraints. This section explores the scalability features and cost considerations for both DynamoDB and PostgreSQL.

1. Scalability

DynamoDB:

- **Automatic Scaling**: DynamoDB is designed with automatic scaling capabilities, allowing it to adjust read and write capacity automatically based on the application's workload. This feature is particularly beneficial for applications with unpredictable traffic patterns, as it ensures that performance remains consistent without manual intervention.
- **Horizontal Scaling**: As a fully managed NoSQL database, DynamoDB can scale horizontally by distributing data across multiple partitions. This allows it to handle large volumes of data and high request rates seamlessly. Users do not need to worry about the underlying infrastructure; AWS manages the partitioning and scaling transparently.
- **Performance Under Load**: DynamoDB is built to deliver low-latency responses even under heavy load, making it suitable for real-time applications such as gaming, IoT, and e-commerce platforms. Its architecture allows it to maintain performance as the dataset grows and the number of concurrent requests increases.

PostgreSQL:

- **Vertical Scaling**: PostgreSQL typically scales vertically, meaning it can benefit from increased hardware resources (e.g., more CPU, RAM, and storage). While this approach can effectively handle increased loads, there are limits to vertical scaling, and hardware upgrades can become costly.

- **Horizontal Scaling Techniques**: Although PostgreSQL is primarily a vertically scalable database, it supports several techniques for horizontal scaling, including:
- **Partitioning**: Large tables can be partitioned into smaller, more manageable pieces, improving query performance and data management.
- **Sharding**: Data can be distributed across multiple PostgreSQL instances, allowing for horizontal scaling. However, implementing sharding often requires additional complexity in managing data distribution and queries across shards.
- **Read Replicas**: PostgreSQL allows the creation of read replicas to offload read traffic from the primary server, improving performance for read-heavy workloads.
- **Performance Considerations**: While PostgreSQL can handle complex queries efficiently, its performance may degrade with highly concurrent workloads. Proper optimization and tuning are essential to maintain performance as the application scales.

Cost Considerations
DynamoDB:

- **Pay-as-You-Go Pricing**: DynamoDB employs a pay-as-you-go pricing model, where costs are based on the provisioned read and write capacity and the amount of data stored. This model can be cost-effective for applications with fluctuating workloads, as users only pay for what they consume.
- **Provisioned Capacity vs. On-Demand Capacity**: Users can choose between provisioned capacity (where they specify the expected read and write throughput) and on-demand capacity (where DynamoDB automatically adjusts capacity based on traffic). On-demand capacity is ideal for applications with unpredictable workloads but may incur higher costs during peak usage.
- **Cost Control Features**: DynamoDB allows users to set limits on maximum capacity and to monitor usage to control costs effectively.

This flexibility enables users to manage their expenses while ensuring consistent performance.

PostgreSQL:

- **Open Source and License-Free**: PostgreSQL is an open-source database, meaning there are no licensing fees associated with its use. However, costs may arise from the infrastructure required to host PostgreSQL, including server hardware, cloud resources, and maintenance.
- **Infrastructure Costs**: The total cost of ownership for PostgreSQL is largely tied to the underlying hardware or cloud resources. Organizations must factor in costs for servers, storage, and backup solutions. Proper planning and optimization can help control these costs.
- **Resource Utilization**: PostgreSQL's cost structure depends on resource utilization. Scaling vertically (upgrading hardware) may involve higher costs, while horizontal scaling (sharding or using read replicas) can distribute costs more effectively. Organizations must balance performance needs with budget constraints.

Choosing the Right Solution

When deciding between DynamoDB and PostgreSQL, consider the following factors related to scalability and cost:

- **Workload Patterns**: If your application experiences unpredictable workloads or requires low-latency responses at scale, DynamoDB's automatic scaling capabilities may be more suitable. Conversely, if your application has steady workloads and requires complex queries and relationships, PostgreSQL may be the better choice.
- **Data Structure**: Consider whether your application requires a flexible schema (DynamoDB) or complex relationships and integrity (PostgreSQL). The chosen data model can influence scalability and cost considerations.

- **Budget Constraints**: Analyze your budget and projected usage patterns. DynamoDB's pay-as-you-go model can be beneficial for applications with variable usage, while PostgreSQL's open-source nature may provide cost advantages for organizations willing to manage infrastructure.

Both DynamoDB and PostgreSQL offer robust scalability options and unique cost structures that cater to different application needs. DynamoDB excels in automatic scaling, low-latency performance, and flexible pricing, making it ideal for high-traffic, real-time applications. PostgreSQL, with its advanced querying capabilities and strong ACID compliance, is well-suited for applications that require complex data management and integrity.

Understanding the scalability features and cost implications of each database system will empower you to make informed decisions that align with your project goals. As we move forward in this book, we will explore practical strategies for leveraging both DynamoDB and PostgreSQL in RESTful API development, ensuring that you can optimize performance and manage costs effectively in your applications.

When to Use Each Database: DynamoDB vs. PostgreSQL

Choosing the right database for your application involves understanding the specific requirements of your project and the strengths of each database system. Both DynamoDB and PostgreSQL have unique characteristics that make them suitable for different use cases. This section provides guidelines on when to use each database based on various factors, including data structure, scalability needs, querying capabilities, and operational considerations.

When to Use DynamoDB

DynamoDB is an excellent choice for applications that require high availability, low latency, and the ability to scale rapidly. Here are specific scenarios where DynamoDB shines:

Real-Time Applications

- **Use Case**: Applications such as gaming, chat applications, and real-time analytics require fast data access and low latency.
- **Reason**: DynamoDB's automatic scaling and optimized performance for key-value access make it ideal for handling real-time workloads where speed is crucial.

High-Volume, Unstructured Data

- **Use Case**: IoT applications, logging systems, or applications dealing with large volumes of user-generated content.
- **Reason**: The key-value store structure allows for flexibility in data schema, making it easy to handle unstructured data without predefined schemas.

Variable Workloads

- **Use Case**: E-commerce platforms that experience fluctuations in traffic (e.g., during sales events or holiday seasons).
- **Reason**: DynamoDB's on-demand capacity mode allows it to automatically adjust to variable workloads, ensuring performance without overspending on capacity.

Simple Query Patterns

- **Use Case**: Applications that primarily access data via unique keys, such as session management or user preferences.
- **Reason**: DynamoDB excels in scenarios where data retrieval is primarily key-based, enabling efficient and fast access.

Serverless Architectures

- **Use Case**: Applications built using AWS Lambda and other serverless services.
- **Reason**: DynamoDB integrates seamlessly with AWS serverless architectures, allowing for easy development and deployment of scalable applications without managing infrastructure.

When to Use PostgreSQL

PostgreSQL is a robust relational database system that excels in scenarios requiring complex querying, data integrity, and structured data management. Here are specific scenarios where PostgreSQL is the preferred choice:

Complex Relationships and Data Integrity

- **Use Case**: Applications that require intricate relationships between data entities, such as financial systems, CRM systems, and ERP solutions.
- **Reason**: PostgreSQL's relational model and support for foreign keys allow for maintaining data integrity and managing complex relationships effectively.

Advanced Querying Needs

- **Use Case**: Applications that require complex queries, reporting, and analytics, such as business intelligence tools and data warehouses.
- **Reason**: PostgreSQL's powerful SQL capabilities, including support for window functions and subqueries, enable sophisticated data analysis and reporting.

Structured Data with Defined Schema

- **Use Case**: Applications that involve structured data with predefined schemas, such as content management systems, e-commerce platforms, and healthcare applications.
- **Reason**: The rigid schema of PostgreSQL ensures data consistency and integrity, making it suitable for applications where data structure is

crucial.

Strong Transactional Requirements

- **Use Case**: Applications that require reliable and atomic transactions, such as banking applications, payment gateways, and inventory management systems.
- **Reason**: PostgreSQL's ACID compliance ensures that transactions are processed reliably, preserving data integrity even in the event of errors.

Geospatial Data Management

- **Use Case**: Applications that require geospatial data processing and analysis, such as mapping services and location-based applications.
- **Reason**: With the PostGIS extension, PostgreSQL can efficiently handle geospatial data and perform complex spatial queries.

Custom Functions and Extensions

- **Use Case**: Applications that require custom logic or functionality, such as specialized analytics or data processing.
- **Reason**: PostgreSQL's extensibility allows developers to create custom functions and use a wide range of available extensions to enhance database capabilities.

Hybrid Approach
In some scenarios, a hybrid approach may be beneficial. For example:

- **Microservices Architecture**: In a microservices architecture, different services can use different databases based on their specific needs. A service that requires low-latency access to unstructured data could use DynamoDB, while another that requires complex queries and strong relationships could use PostgreSQL.

- **Data Lake with Real-Time Analytics**: An application could use DynamoDB for real-time data ingestion from IoT devices while using PostgreSQL for storing historical data and performing complex analytics.

Choosing between DynamoDB and PostgreSQL depends on the specific requirements of your application, including data structure, querying capabilities, performance needs, and operational considerations. DynamoDB is ideal for applications that require scalability, flexibility, and speed, particularly in scenarios involving high traffic and variable workloads. Conversely, PostgreSQL excels in handling complex queries, enforcing data integrity, and managing structured data with defined relationships.

By understanding when to use each database, you can design more efficient and effective data architectures that leverage the strengths of both systems. As we progress through this book, we will delve deeper into implementing and optimizing both DynamoDB and PostgreSQL in RESTful API development, ensuring that you are equipped to make informed decisions for your projects.

Case Studies: Successful Implementations of DynamoDB and PostgreSQL

Understanding how organizations effectively implement DynamoDB and PostgreSQL can provide valuable insights into best practices and practical applications of these database systems. This section presents real-world case studies showcasing successful implementations of both databases, highlighting their strengths and how they solve specific business challenges.

Case Study: Amazon's Use of DynamoDB

Background: Amazon, the company behind DynamoDB, uses this fully managed NoSQL database service extensively across various applications, including its e-commerce platform and streaming services.

Challenge: As a global leader in e-commerce, Amazon handles vast amounts of data and traffic, particularly during peak shopping seasons like Black Friday and Cyber Monday. The challenge was to ensure high availability and performance while managing fluctuating workloads.

Implementation:

- **Automatic Scaling**: Amazon leveraged DynamoDB's automatic scaling feature to adjust read and write capacity based on real-time traffic demands. This allowed the e-commerce platform to handle sudden spikes in user activity without manual intervention.
- **Global Distribution**: DynamoDB's ability to replicate data across multiple AWS regions enabled Amazon to provide low-latency access to its services for users worldwide, enhancing the shopping experience during high-traffic events.

Results:

- **High Availability**: The implementation of DynamoDB ensured that the e-commerce platform remained highly available, with minimal downtime during peak periods.
- **Low Latency**: Users experienced quick load times and responsive interactions, contributing to increased customer satisfaction and sales during critical shopping events.

Case Study: Netflix's Use of PostgreSQL

Background: Netflix, a leading streaming service provider, relies on PostgreSQL for various critical functions, including managing user data, recommendations, and content metadata.

Challenge: As a platform that serves millions of users globally, Netflix needed a database system that could handle complex queries and relationships between users, content, and viewing patterns while ensuring data integrity.

Implementation:

- **Advanced Querying**: Netflix utilized PostgreSQL's rich SQL capabilities to perform complex queries for generating personalized content recommendations based on user viewing history and preferences.
- **Data Integrity**: PostgreSQL's ACID compliance ensured that transactions, such as user sign-ups and subscription changes, were processed reliably without risking data integrity.

Results:

- **Personalized Experience**: The use of PostgreSQL allowed Netflix to deliver tailored recommendations and a personalized viewing experience for its users, enhancing user engagement and retention.
- **Scalability**: PostgreSQL's partitioning and replication features enabled Netflix to scale its database as user demand grew, maintaining performance and availability.

Case Study: Lyft's Use of DynamoDB

Background: Lyft, a prominent ride-sharing platform, uses DynamoDB to manage various aspects of its service, including user requests, driver data, and ride status.

Challenge: With millions of users and drivers interacting in real time, Lyft faced challenges in managing rapid data updates and ensuring that requests were processed quickly and efficiently.

Implementation:

- **Real-Time Data Access**: By leveraging DynamoDB's low-latency performance, Lyft ensured that user requests and driver statuses could be processed in real time, allowing for quick matches between riders and drivers.
- **Data Flexibility**: The key-value data model of DynamoDB provided the flexibility to accommodate evolving data structures, such as new attributes related to rides or user preferences.

Results:

- **Increased Efficiency**: The implementation of DynamoDB led to faster processing of ride requests, reducing wait times for users and improving overall service efficiency.
- **Scalability During Events**: During peak periods, such as major events or holidays, DynamoDB's automatic scaling capabilities enabled Lyft to handle increased demand without compromising performance.

Case Study: The Guardian's Use of PostgreSQL

Background: The Guardian, a leading news organization, utilizes PostgreSQL to manage its content management system and deliver news articles to millions of readers.

Challenge: With a diverse array of articles, multimedia content, and user interactions, The Guardian needed a robust database system to support complex querying and data integrity while managing high traffic.

Implementation:

- **Complex Queries**: The Guardian implemented PostgreSQL's advanced SQL features to efficiently manage and retrieve content, allowing for sophisticated searches and filtering of articles based on various criteria (e.g., topic, author, publication date).
- **Content Relationships**: PostgreSQL's relational model enabled The Guardian to maintain relationships between articles, authors, and categories, facilitating efficient content management and retrieval.

Results:

- **Enhanced User Experience**: The use of PostgreSQL allowed The Guardian to deliver personalized content recommendations and facilitate easy navigation of their vast archive of articles.
- **Reliable Data Management**: The implementation ensured data integrity and reliability, which are essential for maintaining trust in

journalistic content.

Case Study: Spotify's Use of PostgreSQL

Background: Spotify, a popular music streaming service, uses PostgreSQL to manage user accounts, playlists, and metadata about songs and artists.

Challenge: As a platform with millions of active users and an extensive music library, Spotify needed a database system that could efficiently handle complex queries while ensuring data consistency and reliability.

Implementation:

- **User Data Management**: PostgreSQL was used to manage user accounts, preferences, and playlist information. Its ACID compliance ensured that data remained consistent even during high-volume transactions, such as playlist updates.
- **Complex Relationships**: The relational capabilities of PostgreSQL enabled Spotify to efficiently manage relationships between users, songs, and playlists, allowing users to create and share playlists seamlessly.

Results:

- **Scalable Architecture**: The use of PostgreSQL allowed Spotify to scale its database as the user base grew, maintaining performance and responsiveness.
- **Enhanced User Engagement**: The ability to efficiently manage user data and relationships led to improved user experiences and increased engagement on the platform.

These case studies illustrate how organizations across various industries successfully implement DynamoDB and PostgreSQL to address their unique data management challenges. Whether optimizing for low-latency access in real-time applications with DynamoDB or leveraging the robust querying capabilities of PostgreSQL for complex data relationships, these databases provide powerful solutions that enhance application performance and user satisfaction.

As we continue through this book, we will delve deeper into the practical aspects of implementing and optimizing both DynamoDB and PostgreSQL in RESTful API development, equipping you with the knowledge to make informed choices for your applications.

Data Modeling in DynamoDB Techniques

D ata modeling in DynamoDB requires a different approach compared to traditional relational databases due to its key-value structure and NoSQL nature. Effective data modeling is crucial for achieving optimal performance, scalability, and ease of access. This section will cover the concepts of primary keys and secondary indexes in DynamoDB, along with denormalization strategies to enhance data retrieval and storage efficiency.

Primary Keys in DynamoDB

A primary key in DynamoDB uniquely identifies each item within a table and is essential for efficient data retrieval. There are two types of primary keys:

Partition Key

- **Structure**: The partition key consists of a single attribute. When a new item is added to the table, DynamoDB uses the value of the partition key to determine the partition in which to store the item.
- **Uniqueness**: Each item in the table must have a unique partition key value. If two items have the same partition key, they cannot coexist in the same table unless a sort key is also defined.

Example: Consider a user table where the partition key is UserID:

UserID	Name	Email
1001	John	john@example.com
1002	Jane	jane@example.com

Composite Key

- **Structure**: A composite key consists of two attributes: a partition key and a sort key. The combination of these two keys must be unique across all items in the table.
- **Usage**: The partition key groups items, while the sort key allows multiple items with the same partition key to be stored. This structure enables more sophisticated querying and data organization.

Example: In a table of orders, the partition key could be UserID and the sort key could be OrderID:

UserID	OrderID	Product	Quantity
1001	2001	Laptop	1
1001	2002	Smartphone	2
1002	2003	Headphones	3

In this example, the combination of UserID and OrderID uniquely identifies each order.

Secondary Indexes in DynamoDB

Secondary indexes provide additional querying capabilities beyond the primary key. They allow you to retrieve data based on attributes other than the primary key, thus improving flexibility in data access.

Global Secondary Index (GSI)

- **Definition**: A GSI allows you to query data using a different partition key and optional sort key. It can be created on any attribute in the table and is not limited to the primary key.
- **Advantages**: GSIs enable queries that can retrieve items without

scanning the entire table, improving performance for specific access patterns.

Example: Consider a product table where you want to query by Category as well as the ProductID:

ProductID	Name	Category
3001	Laptop	Electronics
3002	T-Shirt	Apparel
3003	Phone	Electronics

You can create a GSI with Category as the partition key, allowing queries like "Get all products in the Electronics category."

Local Secondary Index (LSI)

- **Definition**: An LSI allows querying based on a different sort key while keeping the same partition key. LSIs can only be created at the time of table creation.
- **Advantages**: LSIs enable querying with different sorting options without duplicating data across multiple GSIs.

Example: In the orders table example, if you want to query by UserID and sort orders by OrderDate, you can create an LSI with OrderDate as the sort key:

UserID	OrderID	OrderDate	Product
1001	2001	2024-01-15	Laptop
1001	2002	2024-01-16	Smartphone

Denormalization Strategies

Denormalization is a common practice in NoSQL databases, including DynamoDB, to improve read performance by reducing the need for complex joins or multiple queries. Since DynamoDB does not support joins natively, data is often duplicated across multiple items or tables.

Data Duplication

- **Strategy**: Store related data together within the same item or across different items in the same table to minimize the number of queries required to access related information.
- **Example**: Instead of having a separate table for user profiles and another for orders, you could embed user profile information within each order item:

OrderID	UserID	UserName	Product	Quantity
2001	1001	John	Laptop	1
2002	1001	John	Phone	2

In this example, user profile information (UserName) is duplicated in each order, allowing for easy retrieval of order details along with user information.

Aggregate Data

- **Strategy**: Store precomputed or aggregated data to reduce the need for real-time calculations during queries.
- **Example**: If you frequently need to calculate the total spend per user, you might maintain a separate item that stores this aggregated value:

UserID	TotalSpend
1001	$1500
1002	$750

This approach reduces the need to sum order totals on-the-fly during queries, enhancing performance.

Using Composite Items

- **Strategy**: Store multiple related entities in a single item to optimize data retrieval. This can be effective for one-to-many relationships where it makes sense to retrieve related data together.
- **Example**: For a blogging application, you could store a blog post along with its comments in a single item:

```
{
  "PostID": "1",
  "Title": "My First Post",
  "Content": "This is the content of my first post.",
  "Comments": [
    { "CommentID": "101", "User": "Alice", "Text": "Great post!"
    },
    { "CommentID": "102", "User": "Bob", "Text": "Thanks for
    sharing!" }
  ]
}
```

In this example, retrieving a blog post also retrieves all associated comments, minimizing the number of database calls.

Best Practices for Data Modeling in DynamoDB

To ensure optimal data modeling in DynamoDB, consider the following best practices:

- **Understand Access Patterns**: Design your data model based on anticipated access patterns. Identify the primary queries your application will perform and structure your data accordingly.
- **Use Composite Keys Wisely**: Leverage composite primary keys to manage one-to-many relationships effectively. This approach helps organize data while providing efficient access to related items.
- **Limit the Number of GSIs**: While secondary indexes can enhance

query performance, excessive use can lead to increased costs and complexity. Carefully evaluate the necessity of each GSI.

- **Plan for Future Growth**: Consider how your data model will accommodate future requirements. Design with flexibility in mind, anticipating changes in access patterns or data structure.
- **Monitor Performance**: Regularly review your DynamoDB performance metrics and usage patterns. Adjust your data model and capacity settings based on observed trends and application needs.

Data modeling in DynamoDB requires a thoughtful approach that considers the unique characteristics of the key-value data model. Understanding primary keys, secondary indexes, and denormalization strategies is essential for optimizing data retrieval and ensuring efficient performance. By following best practices and focusing on anticipated access patterns, you can create a robust data model that leverages the strengths of DynamoDB for your applications.

As we move forward in this book, we will explore data modeling techniques in PostgreSQL, highlighting how to effectively design relational databases to meet application needs while ensuring optimal performance and scalability.

Data Modeling in PostgreSQL

Data modeling in PostgreSQL involves designing the database schema to effectively manage and retrieve structured data. This section will discuss normalization techniques and indexing strategies in PostgreSQL, emphasizing how they contribute to data integrity, performance, and efficient data retrieval.

Data Normalization Techniques

Normalization is the process of organizing data within a database to minimize redundancy and improve data integrity. In PostgreSQL, normalization typically involves dividing large tables into smaller, related tables and defining relationships between them. The normalization process follows several normal forms (NF), each with specific rules.

First Normal Form (1NF)

- **Definition**: A table is in 1NF if all its columns contain atomic values (indivisible) and each entry in a column is of the same data type. Additionally, each row must be unique, and there should be no repeating groups or arrays.

Example: A non-normalized table for storing user orders might look like this:

UserID	UserName	Orders
1	John	Order1, Order2
2	Jane	Order3

To convert this table to 1NF, we split the orders into separate rows:

UserID	UserName	Order
1	John	Order1
1	John	Order2
2	Jane	Order3

Second Normal Form (2NF)

- **Definition**: A table is in 2NF if it is in 1NF and all non-key attributes are fully functionally dependent on the primary key. This means that non-key attributes should depend on the entire primary key, not just part of it.

Example: Consider a table with a composite primary key (UserID, OrderID):

UserID	OrderID	UserName	Product
1	101	John	Laptop
1	102	John	Smartphone
2	103	Jane	Headphones

In this case, the UserName attribute depends only on UserID, not on the composite key. To convert this table to 2NF, we separate the user information into a separate table:

Users Table:

UserID	UserName
1	John
2	Jane

Orders Table:

UserID	OrderID	Product
1	101	Laptop
1	102	Smartphone
2	103	Headphones

Third Normal Form (3NF)

- **Definition**: A table is in 3NF if it is in 2NF and all the attributes are functionally dependent only on the primary key. This means that there should be no transitive dependencies (i.e., a non-key attribute should not depend on another non-key attribute).

Example: If the Orders table includes a Supplier attribute that depends on Product, we should eliminate this transitive dependency. We can create a Products table to store product information:

Products Table:

ProductID	Product	Supplier
1	Laptop	SupplierA
2	Smartphone	SupplierB
3	Headphones	SupplierC

Orders Table:

UserID	OrderID	ProductID
1	101	1
1	102	2
2	103	3

Indexing Strategies

Indexing is a critical aspect of optimizing query performance in PostgreSQL. Indexes allow the database to locate and retrieve data more efficiently, reducing the time required for search operations.

Types of Indexes in PostgreSQL

PostgreSQL supports various indexing methods, each designed to optimize performance for different use cases:

- **B-Tree Indexes**: The default index type, suitable for most queries involving equality and range conditions. B-Tree indexes maintain a balanced tree structure, allowing for efficient searching.

Example: Creating a B-Tree index on the UserName column:

```
CREATE INDEX idx_users_username ON users (UserName);
```

- **Hash Indexes**: Useful for equality comparisons, but not suitable for range queries. Hash indexes can be faster than B-Tree for specific use cases but have limitations regarding durability and replication.
- **GIN (Generalized Inverted Index)**: Effective for indexing composite types and full-text search. GIN indexes support complex data types like

arrays and JSONB.

Example: Creating a GIN index on a JSONB column:

```
CREATE INDEX idx_products_attributes ON products USING gin
(attributes);
```

- **GiST (Generalized Search Tree)**: Designed for complex data types such as geometric data. GiST indexes can support a variety of queries, including spatial searches.
- **BRIN (Block Range INdexes)**: Suitable for very large tables where data is stored in a naturally ordered manner. BRIN indexes store summary information about blocks of data, providing space efficiency and performance for certain query types.

Best Practices for Indexing

To maximize the effectiveness of indexing in PostgreSQL, consider the following best practices:

- **Index Selectivity**: Choose columns with high selectivity for indexing. Index selectivity refers to the uniqueness of the column values; highly selective columns (with many unique values) yield better performance.
- **Avoid Over-Indexing**: While indexes improve read performance, they can slow down write operations (INSERT, UPDATE, DELETE). Balance the number of indexes based on your application's read and write patterns.
- **Monitor Index Usage**: Regularly review and monitor index usage statistics to identify unused or underused indexes. This helps to clean up unnecessary indexes that can consume storage and affect performance.
- **Composite Indexes**: Consider using composite indexes when queries involve multiple columns. Composite indexes can be more efficient

than individual indexes for certain query patterns.

Example: Creating a composite index on UserID and OrderDate:

```
CREATE INDEX idx_orders_user_date ON orders (UserID, OrderDate);
```

Data modeling in PostgreSQL is a structured process that emphasizes normalization and efficient indexing strategies. By applying normalization techniques, developers can minimize redundancy and ensure data integrity. Utilizing various indexing strategies allows for optimized query performance, enabling fast data retrieval and improving application responsiveness.

As we continue through this book, we will explore additional data modeling techniques in DynamoDB, highlighting how to effectively design key-value data models to meet application needs while ensuring optimal performance and scalability.

Choosing the Right Model for Your API: DynamoDB vs. PostgreSQL

When designing an API, selecting the appropriate database model is a critical decision that influences the architecture, performance, and scalability of your application. The choice between a key-value data model, like DynamoDB, and a relational data model, such as PostgreSQL, depends on several factors, including the nature of your data, the complexity of your queries, and your application's specific requirements. This section outlines key considerations for choosing the right database model for your API.

1. Understand Your Data Structure

DynamoDB:

- **Key-Value Pair Structure**: If your application primarily requires storing simple data items in a key-value format, DynamoDB is a natural fit. The key-value model is ideal for applications that need rapid access to data using unique identifiers.

- **Unstructured or Semi-Structured Data**: DynamoDB is well-suited for applications that handle unstructured or semi-structured data, such as JSON documents, as it allows for flexible schema design.

PostgreSQL:

- **Structured Data with Relationships**: If your application requires managing structured data with complex relationships, PostgreSQL's relational model is more appropriate. It allows you to define relationships between tables, which is essential for applications that need to enforce data integrity and consistency.
- **Data Normalization**: PostgreSQL's support for normalization techniques makes it suitable for applications that require minimizing redundancy and maintaining data integrity.

Evaluate Query Complexity
DynamoDB:

- **Simple Query Patterns**: If your API will primarily perform simple queries based on primary keys, DynamoDB offers optimal performance with low latency. It excels in scenarios where data retrieval is straightforward and key-based.
- **Limited Query Flexibility**: However, if your application requires complex queries involving joins, aggregations, or filtering across multiple attributes, DynamoDB may not be the best fit due to its limited querying capabilities.

PostgreSQL:

- **Complex Querying Needs**: For applications that require advanced

100

querying capabilities, such as multiple joins, subqueries, and complex filtering, PostgreSQL is the better choice. Its SQL compliance allows for sophisticated queries and reporting.

• **Aggregation and Analytics**: If your API needs to perform aggregation, statistical analysis, or reporting, PostgreSQL's powerful query engine can efficiently handle these tasks.

Consider Scalability Requirements
DynamoDB:

• **Automatic Scaling**: DynamoDB's automatic scaling capabilities make it ideal for applications with unpredictable workloads or those that experience spikes in traffic. It can seamlessly adjust read and write capacity based on demand.

• **Horizontal Scalability**: As a distributed database, DynamoDB is designed to scale horizontally, allowing it to handle large volumes of data and high transaction loads without compromising performance.

PostgreSQL:

• **Vertical Scaling**: PostgreSQL primarily scales vertically, meaning that while you can increase the capacity of your server, there are limits to how far you can scale. This may require significant investment in hardware or cloud resources.

• **Sharding and Partitioning**: While PostgreSQL supports techniques like sharding and partitioning for horizontal scaling, implementing these methods can add complexity to your database management.

Assess Cost Implications
DynamoDB:

• **Pay-as-You-Go Model**: DynamoDB operates on a pay-as-you-go pricing model based on provisioned capacity and storage usage. This model can be advantageous for applications with fluctuating workloads, as costs are directly tied to actual usage.

- **Potential for Higher Costs**: However, if your application has consistently high read/write traffic, costs can add up quickly. It's essential to monitor usage and set capacity limits to manage expenses effectively.

PostgreSQL:

- **No Licensing Fees**: As an open-source database, PostgreSQL does not incur licensing fees, making it cost-effective for organizations. However, you will need to account for the infrastructure and maintenance costs associated with hosting and managing the database.
- **Resource-Based Costs**: The total cost of ownership for PostgreSQL is closely tied to the hardware and resources used. Planning for capacity based on expected growth can help control costs in the long run.

Development and Maintenance Considerations
DynamoDB:

- **Ease of Use**: DynamoDB's managed nature simplifies setup, maintenance, and scaling, allowing developers to focus on building applications rather than managing infrastructure.
- **Learning Curve**: However, developers may need to adapt to the NoSQL paradigm and understand the nuances of key-value data modeling, which can differ significantly from traditional relational models.

PostgreSQL:

- **Familiarity with SQL**: For teams already experienced in SQL and relational database management, PostgreSQL offers a familiar environment. This can reduce the learning curve and speed up development.
- **Maintenance Complexity**: Managing PostgreSQL may involve more

complexity, particularly in scaling, backup, and tuning for performance. Organizations need to allocate resources for database administration.

Choosing the right database model for your API involves careful consideration of your application's data structure, query complexity, scalability needs, cost implications, and maintenance requirements. DynamoDB is an excellent choice for applications requiring rapid access to key-value data, automatic scaling, and flexibility in data structures. In contrast, PostgreSQL is better suited for applications that demand complex queries, data integrity, and structured relationships.

By understanding these factors and aligning them with your project goals, you can make informed decisions that optimize performance and enhance user experience. As we progress through this book, we will further explore best practices for implementing both DynamoDB and PostgreSQL in RESTful API development, ensuring that you can leverage their strengths to deliver effective and efficient solutions.

Building a RESTful API with DynamoDB

Setting Up Your Development Environment
Setting up a development environment is a crucial first step in building a RESTful API with DynamoDB. A well-configured environment ensures that you can efficiently develop, test, and deploy your API. This section outlines the steps necessary to set up your development environment, including installing necessary tools, configuring AWS SDKs, and best practices for organizing your project.

Prerequisites

Before you begin setting up your development environment for building a RESTful API with DynamoDB, ensure that you have the following prerequisites:

- **AWS Account**: Create an AWS account if you don't already have one. You can sign up for a free account on the AWS website.
- **Basic Knowledge of RESTful APIs**: Familiarity with RESTful API principles, HTTP methods (GET, POST, PUT, DELETE), and JSON format will be beneficial.
- **Development Tools**: Have a code editor (e.g., Visual Studio Code, Sublime Text) and command-line interface (CLI) tools installed.

Installing Development Tools

To build a RESTful API, you'll need to install several development tools. Here's a list of essential tools:

AWS Command Line Interface (CLI)

The AWS CLI allows you to interact with AWS services, including DynamoDB, from the command line. To install the AWS CLI:

Download and Install:

- For Windows, download the installer from the AWS CLI documentation.
- For macOS, you can use Homebrew:

```
brew install awscli
```

- For Linux, you can use pip:

```
pip install awscli --upgrade --user
```

Configure AWS CLI: After installation, configure the AWS CLI with your AWS credentials:

```
aws configure
```

You will be prompted to enter your AWS Access Key ID, Secret Access Key, region, and output format (typically json).

Node.js and npm

If you plan to use Node.js to build your RESTful API, you need to install Node.js, which includes npm (Node Package Manager).

Download and Install: Visit the Node.js website and download the installer for your operating system. Follow the installation instructions.

Verify Installation: After installation, verify that Node.js and npm are installed by running:

```
node -v
npm -v
```

Express Framework

Express is a popular web framework for Node.js that simplifies the process of building RESTful APIs.

Install Express: Create a new directory for your project and navigate to it in the terminal. Initialize a new Node.js project and install Express:

```
mkdir my-api
cd my-api
npm init -y
npm install express
```

AWS SDK for JavaScript

The AWS SDK for JavaScript allows you to interact with AWS services, including DynamoDB, directly from your Node.js application.

Install AWS SDK: In your project directory, install the AWS SDK:

```
npm install aws-sdk
```

Setting Up Your Project Structure

Organizing your project structure effectively will help maintain clarity and manageability as your application grows. Here's a suggested directory structure for your RESTful API:

```
my-api/   │  ├───
```

```
node_modules/          # Contains installed npm packages ├──────
src/                   # Application source code │ ├────────
    controllers/       # Controller functions to handle
    requests │ ├───────
    models/            # Data models and schemas │ ├────────
    routes/            # API routes │ ├───────
    services/          # Business logic and service
    functions │ ├───────
    config/            # Configuration files (AWS settings,
    environment variables) │ └──────
    index.js           # Entry point for the
    application │ ├───────

.env                   # Environment variables (e.g., AWS
credentials) ├──────
package.json           # npm configuration file └──────
README.md              # Project documentation
```

Creating a Basic Server with Express

To set up a basic RESTful API server using Express, follow these steps:

Create the Entry Point

Create index.js: In the src directory, create a file named index.js. This file will serve as the entry point for your application.

Basic Server Setup: Add the following code to index.js to set up a basic Express server:

```
const express = require('express');
const app = express();
const port = process.env.PORT || 3000;

// Middleware to parse JSON requests
app.use(express.json());

// Sample route
```

```
app.get('/', (req, res) => {
    res.send('Welcome to the DynamoDB RESTful API!');
});

// Start the server
app.listen(port, () => {
    console.log(`Server is running on http://localhost:${port}`);
});
```

Run the Server

1. **Start the Server**: In the terminal, navigate to your project directory and run:

```
node src/index.js
```

Test the API: Open a web browser or use a tool like Postman to test the API by navigating to http://localhost:3000. You should see the welcome message.

Configuring Environment Variables

Using environment variables helps you manage sensitive information (like AWS credentials) and configuration settings without hardcoding them into your application.

Create a .env File: In the root of your project directory, create a file named .env.

Add AWS Configuration: Add your AWS Access Key ID, Secret Access Key, and region to the .env file:

```
AWS_ACCESS_KEY_ID=your_access_key_id
AWS_SECRET_ACCESS_KEY=your_secret_access_key
AWS_REGION=your_region
```

Install dotenv Package: To load environment variables from the .env file, install the dotenv package:

```
npm install dotenv
```

Load Environment Variables: Update your index.js file to load the environment variables:

```
require('dotenv').config();

const express = require('express');
const app = express();
const port = process.env.PORT || 3000;

app.use(express.json());

// Sample route
app.get('/', (req, res) => {
    res.send('Welcome to the DynamoDB RESTful API!');
});

// Start the server
app.listen(port, () => {
    console.log(`Server is running on http://localhost:${port}`);
});
```

Best Practices for Development Environment Setup

To ensure a smooth development experience, consider the following best practices:

- **Version Control**: Use a version control system (e.g., Git) to manage your codebase. This allows you to track changes, collaborate with others, and revert to previous versions if needed.
- **Documentation**: Maintain a README.md file to document your project setup, dependencies, and usage instructions. This is especially

useful for onboarding new team members.

- **Consistent Environment**: Use tools like Docker to create a consistent development environment that can be easily replicated across different machines.
- **Testing**: Incorporate testing tools (e.g., Mocha, Chai, Jest) into your development environment to ensure code quality and functionality as you build your API.

Setting up your development environment is a critical step in building a RESTful API with DynamoDB. By installing necessary tools, organizing your project structure, and configuring your application, you lay a solid foundation for efficient development. Following best practices will help streamline your workflow, ensuring that your API development process is productive and manageable.

As we move forward in this book, we will delve into implementing the various components of your RESTful API, including routes, controllers, and integration with DynamoDB, allowing you to build a fully functional application.

Creating Your First API Endpoint

Once your development environment is set up, the next step is to create your first API endpoint. This section will guide you through the process of setting up an endpoint in your Express application, integrating it with DynamoDB to perform basic CRUD (Create, Read, Update, Delete) operations.

Setting Up DynamoDB

Before creating your API endpoint, ensure that you have set up a DynamoDB table where your data will be stored. For this example, let's create a simple table to store user information.

Creating a DynamoDB Table

Access the AWS Management Console: Log in to your AWS account and navigate to the DynamoDB service.

Create a New Table:

- Click on **Create Table**.
- **Table Name**: Enter Users.
- **Primary Key**: Set the partition key to UserID (String).
- **Leave other options as default** and click **Create**.

Verify the Table: After the table is created, you should see it listed in the DynamoDB console.

Installing AWS SDK for JavaScript

You've already installed the AWS SDK in your development environment. Ensure you have it properly configured to interact with DynamoDB.

Import AWS SDK: In your index.js file (or a new file if you prefer), import the AWS SDK and configure it to use your credentials:

```
const AWS = require('aws-sdk');
require('dotenv').config();

// Configure the AWS SDK
AWS.config.update({
    region: process.env.AWS_REGION,
    accessKeyId: process.env.AWS_ACCESS_KEY_ID,
    secretAccessKey: process.env.AWS_SECRET_ACCESS_KEY
});

const dynamoDB = new AWS.DynamoDB.DocumentClient();
```

Creating Your First API Endpoint

Now that you have your DynamoDB table set up and the AWS SDK configured, you can create your first API endpoint to add a user.

Adding the POST Endpoint

Define the Route: In your index.js file, set up a POST endpoint for creating a new user. Below is an example of how to do this:

```
app.post('/users', async (req, res) => {
    const { UserID, UserName, Email } = req.body;

    const params = {
        TableName: 'Users',
        Item: {
            UserID,
            UserName,
            Email
        }
    };

    try {
        await dynamoDB.put(params).promise();
        res.status(201).json({ message: 'User created
        successfully', UserID });
    } catch (error) {
        console.error('Error creating user:', error);
        res.status(500).json({ error: 'Could not create user' });
    }
});
```

Explanation:

- The route /users listens for POST requests to create new users.
- The user data is extracted from the request body (req.body).
- A params object is created to define the TableName and the Item to be added to DynamoDB.
- The put method of the DocumentClient is used to insert the new user. If the operation is successful, a success message is returned with a 201 status code. If there's an error, a 500 status code is returned.

Testing the Endpoint

Start Your Server: If your server isn't already running, start it by running:

```
node src/index.js
```

Use Postman to Test:

- Open Postman and set the request type to POST.
- Enter the URL: http://localhost:3000/users.
- In the **Body** tab, select **raw** and set the type to **JSON**. Enter the following JSON:

```
{
    "UserID": "1001",
    "UserName": "John Doe",
    "Email": "john.doe@example.com"
}
```

- Click **Send**.

Check the Response: You should receive a response indicating that the user was created successfully. The response should look like this:

```
{
    "message": "User created successfully",
    "UserID": "1001"
}
```

Verify in DynamoDB: Navigate back to the DynamoDB console, and check the Users table to verify that the new user has been added.

Creating a GET Endpoint

Next, let's create a GET endpoint to retrieve user information.

4.1 Define the GET Route

Add the following code to create a GET endpoint for retrieving user data:

```
app.get('/users/:UserID', async (req, res) => {
    const { UserID } = req.params;

    const params = {
        TableName: 'Users',
        Key: {
            UserID
        }
    };

    try {
        const result = await dynamoDB.get(params).promise();
        if (result.Item) {
            res.status(200).json(result.Item);
        } else {
            res.status(404).json({ error: 'User not found' });
        }
    } catch (error) {
        console.error('Error retrieving user:', error);
        res.status(500).json({ error: 'Could not retrieve user'
        });
    }
});
```

Explanation:

- This endpoint listens for GET requests to /users/:UserID, where :UserID is a path parameter.
- It retrieves the user information based on the provided UserID.
- If the user is found, it returns the user data with a 200 status code. If not, it returns a 404 status code.

Testing the GET Endpoint

1. **Use Postman to Test:**

- Set the request type to GET.
- Enter the URL: http://localhost:3000/users/1001.
- Click **Send**.

1. **Check the Response**: You should receive the user information as a JSON response:

```
{
    "UserID": "1001",
    "UserName": "John Doe",
    "Email": "john.doe@example.com"
}
```

You have successfully created your first API endpoints for a RESTful API using DynamoDB and Express. You learned how to set up a POST endpoint to create a new user and a GET endpoint to retrieve user information. These fundamental operations form the backbone of a RESTful API and set the stage for further development.

As you continue building your API, you can implement additional endpoints for updating and deleting users, as well as expanding the functionality to include more complex operations and features. In the following chapters, we will explore advanced features such as error handling, input validation, and best practices for securing your API, ensuring a robust and scalable application.

CRUD Operations with DynamoDB

CRUD operations (Create, Read, Update, Delete) are the foundational actions for managing data in any database, including DynamoDB. In this section, we will explore how to implement these operations in your RESTful API using DynamoDB, ensuring you can effectively manage user data in your application.

Create Operation

The Create operation allows you to add new items to a DynamoDB table. In our example, we will continue with the Users table.

Implementing the Create Endpoint

We have already implemented the POST endpoint for creating a new user in the previous chapter. For reference, here's the code again:

```
app.post('/users', async (req, res) => {
    const { UserID, UserName, Email } = req.body;

    const params = {
        TableName: 'Users',
        Item: {
            UserID,
            UserName,
            Email
        }
    };

    try {
        await dynamoDB.put(params).promise();
        res.status(201).json({ message: 'User created
        successfully', UserID });
    } catch (error) {
        console.error('Error creating user:', error);
        res.status(500).json({ error: 'Could not create user' });
    }
});
```

Read Operation

The Read operation retrieves data from the database. We have already created a GET endpoint to retrieve a user by their UserID. Here's a quick refresher:

Implementing the Read Endpoint

```
app.get('/users/:UserID', async (req, res) => {
    const { UserID } = req.params;

    const params = {
        TableName: 'Users',
        Key: {
            UserID
        }
    };

    try {
        const result = await dynamoDB.get(params).promise();
        if (result.Item) {
            res.status(200).json(result.Item);
        } else {
            res.status(404).json({ error: 'User not found' });
        }
    } catch (error) {
        console.error('Error retrieving user:', error);
        res.status(500).json({ error: 'Could not retrieve user'
        });
    }
});
```

Update Operation

The Update operation modifies an existing item in the DynamoDB table. You can specify which attributes to update without having to resend the entire item.

Implementing the Update Endpoint

Add the PUT Endpoint: Create a new endpoint for updating user information:

```
app.put('/users/:UserID', async (req, res) => {
```

117

```
const { UserID } = req.params;
const { UserName, Email } = req.body;

const params = {
    TableName: 'Users',
    Key: {
        UserID
    },
    UpdateExpression: 'SET UserName = :name, Email = :email',
    ExpressionAttributeValues: {
        ':name': UserName,
        ':email': Email
    },
    ReturnValues: 'UPDATED_NEW'
};

try {
    const result = await dynamoDB.update(params).promise();
    if (result.Attributes) {
        res.status(200).json({ message: 'User updated
        successfully', User: result.Attributes });
    } else {
        res.status(404).json({ error: 'User not found' });
    }
} catch (error) {
    console.error('Error updating user:', error);
    res.status(500).json({ error: 'Could not update user' });
}
});
```

Explanation:

- The PUT endpoint listens for requests to /users/:UserID to update user information.
- The UpdateExpression specifies the attributes to update, and Expressio nAttributeValues provides the new values.
- The ReturnValues parameter allows you to return the updated item.

Delete Operation

The Delete operation removes an item from the database based on its key.

Implementing the Delete Endpoint

Add the DELETE Endpoint: Create a new endpoint for deleting a user:

```
app.delete('/users/:UserID', async (req, res) => {
    const { UserID } = req.params;

    const params = {
        TableName: 'Users',
        Key: {
            UserID
        }
    };

    try {
        await dynamoDB.delete(params).promise();
        res.status(204).send();  // No content returned
    } catch (error) {
        console.error('Error deleting user:', error);
        res.status(500).json({ error: 'Could not delete user' });
    }
});
```

Explanation:

- The DELETE endpoint listens for requests to /users/:UserID to remove a user.
- Upon successful deletion, a 204 status code is returned, indicating that the operation was successful and there is no content to return.

Testing the CRUD Operations

Once you have implemented all the CRUD operations, it's essential to test them to ensure they work correctly. Use Postman or a similar tool to perform the following tests:

Testing Create Operation

119

- Send a POST request to http://localhost:3000/users with a JSON body to create a new user.

Testing Read Operation

- Send a GET request to http://localhost:3000/users/1001 (or the UserID you created) to retrieve user information.

Testing Update Operation

- Send a PUT request to http://localhost:3000/users/1001 with a JSON body to update user information.

Testing Delete Operation

- Send a DELETE request to http://localhost:3000/users/1001 to delete the user.

Best Practices for CRUD Operations

To ensure efficient and effective CRUD operations in your DynamoDB-based API, consider the following best practices:

- **Input Validation**: Always validate incoming data to ensure it meets the expected format and constraints before processing it. This helps prevent errors and potential security vulnerabilities.
- **Error Handling**: Implement robust error handling to manage exceptions and return meaningful error messages. This improves the API's usability and helps clients troubleshoot issues.
- **Consistent Responses**: Maintain a consistent structure for API responses, including success and error responses. This simplifies client-side processing and enhances the overall user experience.
- **Use Strong Consistency Where Necessary**: For critical read operations that require the most up-to-date data, consider using strongly

consistent reads in DynamoDB, understanding that this may impact performance.

- **Optimize Data Access Patterns**: Analyze your application's data access patterns and design your DynamoDB table accordingly, leveraging partition and sort keys effectively.

You have successfully implemented CRUD operations in your RESTful API using DynamoDB. By creating endpoints for creating, reading, updating, and deleting users, you have laid the foundation for managing user data effectively. Testing these endpoints ensures that they function correctly and provides a solid user experience.

As we progress through this book, we will delve into advanced topics such as implementing authentication and authorization, optimizing performance, and managing data access patterns in your RESTful API. These additional features will enhance the robustness and security of your application.

Handling Errors and Validations in a RESTful API with DynamoDB

Effective error handling and input validation are crucial components of building a robust RESTful API. They ensure that your API can gracefully manage unexpected situations and maintain data integrity. In this section, we will explore best practices for error handling and input validation when working with DynamoDB and Express.

Importance of Error Handling

Error handling is essential for:

- **User Experience**: Providing clear feedback to users when something goes wrong helps improve their experience and enables them to take corrective action.
- **Debugging and Maintenance**: Logging errors and providing detailed messages can help developers identify and fix issues more quickly.
- **Data Integrity**: Proper error handling ensures that data operations are

executed correctly and helps maintain the integrity of your database.

Common Error Types

When building a RESTful API, you may encounter various types of errors. Here are some common error categories:

- **Client Errors (4xx)**: These errors indicate that the client made a bad request. Common examples include:
- 400 Bad Request: The request could not be understood due to malformed syntax.
- 404 Not Found: The requested resource does not exist (e.g., trying to retrieve a user that does not exist).
- 409 Conflict: There is a conflict with the current state of the resource (e.g., attempting to create a user with an existing UserID).
- **Server Errors (5xx)**: These errors indicate that the server failed to fulfill a valid request. Common examples include:
- 500 Internal Server Error: An unexpected condition prevented the server from fulfilling the request.

Implementing Error Handling in Express

You can implement error handling in Express using middleware functions and try-catch blocks. Here's how to do it effectively:

3.1 Global Error Handling Middleware

Create a global error-handling middleware to catch errors that occur during request processing. Add this middleware after defining your routes:

```
// Error handling middleware
app.use((err, req, res, next) => {
    console.error(err.message);
    res.status(err.status || 500).json({ error: err.message });
});
```

Try-Catch Blocks for Async Operations

For asynchronous operations (such as database queries), use try-catch blocks to handle potential errors:

```
app.post('/users', async (req, res, next) => {
    const { UserID, UserName, Email } = req.body;

    const params = {
        TableName: 'Users',
        Item: {
            UserID,
            UserName,
            Email
        }
    };

    try {
        await dynamoDB.put(params).promise();
        res.status(201).json({ message: 'User created
        successfully', UserID });
    } catch (error) {
        console.error('Error creating user:', error);
        error.status = 500; // Set custom status code
        next(error); // Pass the error to the error-handling
        middleware
    }
});
```

Input Validation

Input validation is essential to ensure that incoming data meets expected formats and constraints before processing it. This helps prevent errors and maintain data integrity.

Using a Validation Library

To simplify input validation, consider using a library like Joi or express-validator. Here's how to set up input validation with Joi:

Install Joi:

```
npm install joi
```

Define a Validation Schema:

Create a validation schema for the user data in a separate file (e.g., validator s/userValidator.js):

```
const Joi = require('joi');

const userSchema = Joi.object({
    UserID: Joi.string().required(),
    UserName: Joi.string().min(3).max(30).required(),
    Email: Joi.string().email().required()
});

module.exports = userSchema;
```

Integrate Validation into Your Endpoint:

In your API endpoint, use the validation schema to validate incoming data:

```
const userSchema = require('./validators/userValidator');

app.post('/users', async (req, res, next) => {
    const { error } = userSchema.validate(req.body);

    if (error) {
        return res.status(400).json({ error:
        error.details[0].message });
    }

    const { UserID, UserName, Email } = req.body;

    const params = {
        TableName: 'Users',
```

```
    Item: {
        UserID,
        UserName,
        Email
    }
};

try {
    await dynamoDB.put(params).promise();
    res.status(201).json({ message: 'User created
    successfully', UserID });
} catch (error) {
    console.error('Error creating user:', error);
    error.status = 500; // Set custom status code
    next(error); // Pass the error to the error-handling
    middleware
}
});
```

Custom Error Handling Logic

For specific error cases, you can implement custom logic to handle known errors gracefully. For instance, if a user tries to create a user with an existing UserID, you can check for this condition and respond with a meaningful message:

```
app.post('/users', async (req, res, next) => {
    const { error } = userSchema.validate(req.body);

    if (error) {
        return res.status(400).json({ error:
        error.details[0].message });
    }

    const { UserID, UserName, Email } = req.body;

    const checkUserParams = {
        TableName: 'Users',
```

```
        Key: { UserID }
    };

    try {
        const existingUser = await
        dynamoDB.get(checkUserParams).promise();

        if (existingUser.Item) {
            return res.status(409).json({ error: 'UserID already
            exists' });
        }

        const params = {
            TableName: 'Users',
            Item: { UserID, UserName, Email }
        };

        await dynamoDB.put(params).promise();
        res.status(201).json({ message: 'User created
        successfully', UserID });
    } catch (error) {
        console.error('Error creating user:', error);
        error.status = 500; // Set custom status code
        next(error); // Pass the error to the error-handling
        middleware
    }
});
```

Logging Errors

Logging errors is essential for debugging and monitoring your application. Use a logging library like winston or morgan to keep track of errors and application activity.

Install Winston:

```
npm install winston
```

Set Up Winston: In your index.js, configure Winston for logging:

```
const winston = require('winston');

const logger = winston.createLogger({
    level: 'info',
    format: winston.format.json(),
    transports: [
        new winston.transports.Console(),
        new winston.transports.File({ filename: 'error.log',
        level: 'error' })
    ]
});

// Example usage in an error handling middleware
app.use((err, req, res, next) => {
    logger.error(err.message);
    res.status(err.status || 500).json({ error: err.message });
});
```

Handling errors and validating input are vital for building a robust RESTful API with DynamoDB. By implementing effective error-handling strategies and validating incoming data, you can ensure that your API operates reliably and securely, enhancing the user experience.

In this chapter, you learned how to set up global error handling in Express, implement input validation using Joi, and manage specific error cases effectively. Additionally, you explored the importance of logging errors for debugging and monitoring purposes.

As we continue through this book, we will delve into more advanced topics, such as authentication and authorization, securing your API, and implementing best practices for performance and scalability. These elements will further enhance the reliability and usability of your RESTful API.

Testing Your API

Testing is a crucial part of the development process for any RESTful API. It helps ensure that your API behaves as expected, functions correctly under various conditions, and can handle errors gracefully. This section will cover different methods of testing your API, including manual testing with tools like Postman, automated testing with frameworks like Mocha and Chai, and best practices for effective testing.

Importance of API Testing

- **Verifying Functionality**: Testing confirms that each API endpoint works as intended and that the expected data is returned for given inputs.
- **Ensuring Reliability**: By performing tests, you can identify bugs and issues early in the development process, ensuring the API is reliable for users.
- **Performance and Load Testing**: Assessing how the API behaves under load is essential for understanding its performance and scalability.
- **Documentation**: Tests can serve as a form of documentation, showcasing how the API is expected to behave under different conditions.

Manual Testing with Postman

Postman is a popular tool for manually testing APIs. It provides a user-friendly interface for sending requests to your API and examining the responses.

Setting Up Postman

Download and Install Postman: You can download Postman from the official website.

Create a New Request:

- Open Postman and create a new request by clicking on the "+" button.
- Set the request type (GET, POST, PUT, DELETE) based on the endpoint you want to test.
- Enter the URL of your API endpoint (e.g., http://localhost:3000/users).

Testing CRUD Operations

- **Testing Create Operation**:
- Select POST as the request type.
- Set the URL to http://localhost:3000/users.
- In the Body tab, select raw and choose JSON. Enter the JSON data for a new user:

```
{
    "UserID": "1001",
    "UserName": "John Doe",
    "Email": "john.doe@example.com"
}
```

- Click Send and check the response for a success message.
- **Testing Read Operation**:
- Select GET as the request type.
- Set the URL to http://localhost:3000/users/1001.
- Click Send and verify that the correct user data is returned.
- **Testing Update Operation**:
- Select PUT as the request type.
- Set the URL to http://localhost:3000/users/1001.
- In the Body tab, provide updated JSON data:

```
{
    "UserName": "John Smith",
    "Email": "john.smith@example.com"
}
```

- Click Send and check the response for a success message.
- **Testing Delete Operation**:
- Select DELETE as the request type.
- Set the URL to http://localhost:3000/users/1001.
- Click Send and confirm that the response status is 204 (No Content).

Automated Testing with Mocha and Chai

Automated testing helps streamline the testing process, allowing you to run multiple tests quickly and consistently.

Setting Up Mocha and Chai

Install Mocha and Chai: In your project directory, install Mocha (test framework) and Chai (assertion library):

```
npm install --save-dev mocha chai chai-http
```

Create a Test Directory: Create a directory for your tests (e.g., test) in your project root.

Create a Test File: Inside the test directory, create a file named users.test.js.

Writing Tests

Here's a basic example of how to write tests for your API using Mocha and Chai:

```
const chai = require('chai');
const chaiHttp = require('chai-http');
const app = require('../src/index'); // Import your Express app
const expect = chai.expect;

chai.use(chaiHttp);

describe('User API', () => {
    it('should create a new user', (done) => {
```

```
    chai.request(app)
        .post('/users')
        .send({ UserID: '1001', UserName: 'John Doe', Email:
        'john.doe@example.com' })
        .end((err, res) => {
            expect(res).to.have.status(201);
            expect(res.body).to.have.property('message',
            'User created successfully');
            done();
        });
});

it('should retrieve a user by ID', (done) => {
    chai.request(app)
        .get('/users/1001')
        .end((err, res) => {
            expect(res).to.have.status(200);
            expect(res.body).to.have.property('UserID',
            '1001');
            expect(res.body).to.have.property('UserName',
            'John Doe');
            done();
        });
});

it('should update a user', (done) => {
    chai.request(app)
        .put('/users/1001')
        .send({ UserName: 'John Smith', Email:
        'john.smith@example.com' })
        .end((err, res) => {
            expect(res).to.have.status(200);
            expect(res.body).to.have.property('message',
            'User updated successfully');
            done();
        });
});

it('should delete a user', (done) => {
    chai.request(app)
```

```
            .delete('/users/1001')
            .end((err, res) => {
                expect(res).to.have.status(204);
                done();
            });
    });
});
```

Running the Tests

Modify package.json: Add a test script to your package.json file:

```
"scripts": {
    "test": "mocha"
}
```

Run the Tests: Execute the following command in your terminal:

```
npm test
```

You should see the results of your tests in the terminal. Each test case will indicate whether it passed or failed, providing feedback on the correctness of your API endpoints.

Best Practices for API Testing

To ensure effective testing of your API, consider the following best practices:

- **Test Coverage**: Aim for comprehensive test coverage that includes all endpoints and possible scenarios, including edge cases and error conditions.
- **Use Test Data**: When writing tests, use test data that mimics real-world scenarios. Consider using fixtures or factories to generate consistent test data.

- **Automate Tests**: Automate your tests as much as possible to save time and ensure consistency. Set up continuous integration (CI) tools to run your tests automatically whenever changes are made.
- **Monitor Performance**: In addition to functional testing, consider performance testing to assess how your API behaves under load. Tools like Apache JMeter or Artillery can help simulate traffic and measure response times.
- **Document Test Cases**: Keep a record of your test cases, including expected inputs and outputs. This documentation can be useful for onboarding new team members and ensuring consistent testing practices.

Testing your API is a vital step in ensuring its reliability and performance. By utilizing tools like Postman for manual testing and frameworks like Mocha and Chai for automated testing, you can ensure that your RESTful API operates as expected and is prepared for real-world usage.

In this chapter, you learned how to set up both manual and automated tests for your CRUD operations, along with best practices for effective API testing. As we progress further in this book, we will explore advanced topics such as securing your API, implementing authentication and authorization, and optimizing performance to ensure that your application is robust, secure, and scalable.

Building a RESTful API with PostgreSQL

Setting Up Your Development Environment
Setting up a development environment for building a RESTful API with PostgreSQL involves several key steps. This section will guide you through the installation of essential tools, configuring PostgreSQL, and best practices for organizing your project structure. By the end, you'll have a fully prepared environment for developing your API.

Prerequisites

Before you start setting up your development environment, ensure you have the following prerequisites:

- **PostgreSQL Account**: If you don't have PostgreSQL installed, you can either download it locally or use a managed service like Amazon RDS.
- **Basic Knowledge of RESTful APIs**: Familiarity with RESTful principles, HTTP methods (GET, POST, PUT, DELETE), and JSON format will be beneficial.
- **Development Tools**: Have a code editor (e.g., Visual Studio Code, Sublime Text) and command-line interface (CLI) tools installed.

Installing PostgreSQL

To set up PostgreSQL, follow the steps for your specific operating system:

Windows

Download the Installer: Go to the PostgreSQL official website and download the installer for Windows.

Run the Installer: Follow the installation wizard, selecting the components you need (including pgAdmin for database management).

Set Password: During installation, you will be prompted to set a password for the postgres superuser. Make sure to remember this password.

macOS

Using Homebrew: If you have Homebrew installed, you can easily install PostgreSQL by running:

```
brew install postgresql
```

Start PostgreSQL Service: After installation, start the PostgreSQL service:

```
brew services start postgresql
```

Linux

Using APT for Ubuntu/Debian:

```
sudo apt update
sudo apt install postgresql postgresql-contrib
```

Using YUM for CentOS/RHEL:

```
sudo yum install postgresql-server postgresql-contrib
```

Initialize the Database (if required):

```
sudo postgresql-setup initdb
```

Start PostgreSQL Service:

```
sudo systemctl start postgresql
```

Configuring PostgreSQL

After installation, you need to configure PostgreSQL and create a database for your API.

Accessing PostgreSQL

Open Terminal or Command Prompt: Depending on your operating system, open a terminal or command prompt.

Access the PostgreSQL Command Line: Switch to the PostgreSQL user and access the command line interface:

```
psql -U postgres
```

Enter Your Password: When prompted, enter the password you set during installation.

Creating a Database

Once in the PostgreSQL command line, create a new database for your API:

```
CREATE DATABASE my_api;
```

You can check that the database was created successfully by running:

```
\l
```

This command lists all databases, including the one you just created.

Creating a User

Create a new user with privileges to access your database:

```sql
Copy code
CREATE USER api_user WITH PASSWORD 'your_password';
```

Grant the user permissions to access the database:

```
GRANT ALL PRIVILEGES ON DATABASE my_api TO api_user;
```

Exiting PostgreSQL

To exit the PostgreSQL command line, type:

```
\q
```

Installing Development Tools

In addition to PostgreSQL, you'll need several development tools to build your RESTful API effectively.

Node.js and npm

If you plan to use Node.js for your API, you need to install Node.js and npm:

1. **Download and Install**: Visit the Node.js website and download the installer for your operating system.
2. **Verify Installation**:

```bash
Copy code
node -v
npm -v
```

Express Framework

Express is a minimalist web framework for Node.js that simplifies the creation of web applications and APIs.

Create a New Directory:

```
mkdir my-postgres-api
cd my-postgres-api
```

Initialize a New Node.js Project:

```
npm init -y
```

Install Express:

```
npm install express
```

Sequelize ORM

Sequelize is a promise-based Node.js ORM for PostgreSQL that provides an easy way to interact with your database.

Install Sequelize and PostgreSQL Driver:

```
npm install sequelize pg pg-hstore
```

Setting Up Your Project Structure

A well-organized project structure enhances maintainability and readability. Here's a suggested directory structure for your RESTful API:

```
my-postgres-api/ │ ├──────

  node_modules/          # Contains installed npm packages ├──────
  src/                   # Application source code │ ├──────
    controllers/         # Controller functions to handle
    requests │ ├──────
    models/              # Sequelize models for database
    tables │ ├──────
    routes/              # API routes │ ├──────
    config/              # Configuration files (database
    settings) │ └──────
    index.js             # Entry point for the
    application │ ├──────

  .env                   # Environment variables (e.g., database
  credentials) ├──────
  package.json           # npm configuration file └──────
  README.md              # Project documentation
```

Creating a Basic Server with Express

To set up a basic Express server that connects to PostgreSQL, follow these steps:

Create the Entry Point

Create index.js: In the src directory, create a file named index.js.

Basic Server Setup: Add the following code to index.js to set up a basic Express server and connect to PostgreSQL:

```
const express = require('express');
const { Sequelize } = require('sequelize');
require('dotenv').config();

const app = express();
const port = process.env.PORT || 3000;
```

```
// Middleware to parse JSON requests
app.use(express.json());

// Connect to PostgreSQL
const sequelize = new Sequelize(process.env.DATABASE_URL, {
    dialect: 'postgres',
    logging: false,
});

// Test the connection
sequelize.authenticate()
    .then(() => {
        console.log('Connection to PostgreSQL has been
        established successfully.');
    })
    .catch(err => {
        console.error('Unable to connect to the database:', err);
    });

// Sample route
app.get('/', (req, res) => {
    res.send('Welcome to the PostgreSQL RESTful API!');
});

// Start the server
app.listen(port, () => {
    console.log(`Server is running on http://localhost:${port}`);
});
```

Creating the .env File

To manage sensitive information, create a .env file in the root of your project directory:

```
DATABASE_URL=postgres://api_user:your_password@localhost:5432/my_api
```

Replace your_password with the actual password you set for api_user.

Best Practices for Development Environment Setup

To ensure a smooth development experience, consider the following best practices:

- **Version Control**: Use a version control system (e.g., Git) to manage your codebase. This allows you to track changes, collaborate with others, and revert to previous versions if needed.
- **Documentation**: Maintain a README.md file to document your project setup, dependencies, and usage instructions. This is especially useful for onboarding new team members.
- **Consistent Environment**: Use tools like Docker to create a consistent development environment that can be easily replicated across different machines.
- **Testing**: Incorporate testing tools (e.g., Mocha, Chai) into your development environment to ensure code quality and functionality as you build your API.

Setting up your development environment for building a RESTful API with PostgreSQL is a crucial step in the development process. By installing necessary tools, configuring PostgreSQL, and organizing your project structure, you lay a solid foundation for efficient API development.

In the next chapters, we will delve into implementing the various components of your RESTful API, including routes, controllers, and integration with PostgreSQL, allowing you to build a fully functional application. We will also explore advanced features such as error handling, validation, and testing, ensuring that your API is robust, secure, and scalable.

Creating Your First API Endpoint

Now that your development environment is set up and your PostgreSQL database is configured, the next step is to create your first API endpoint.

In this section, we will walk through the process of setting up an endpoint in your Express application to handle user data, specifically focusing on creating, reading, updating, and deleting users.

Setting Up Your Database Table

Before creating the API endpoint, ensure that you have a Users table in your PostgreSQL database. You can create this table using the following SQL command.

Creating the Users Table

Access PostgreSQL: Open your terminal and connect to your PostgreSQL database:

```
psql -U api_user -d my_api
```

Create the Table: Run the following SQL command to create a Users table:

```
CREATE TABLE Users (
    UserID SERIAL PRIMARY KEY,
    UserName VARCHAR(50) NOT NULL,
    Email VARCHAR(100) NOT NULL UNIQUE
);
```

Verify the Table: After running the command, you can check that the table was created successfully by running:

```
\dt
```

This command lists all tables in the current database, including the newly created Users table.

Creating Your First API Endpoint

Now that you have the database table set up, you can create your first API endpoint. We will start with a POST endpoint to create a new user.

Adding the POST Endpoint

Update Your Express Application: Open your index.js file in the src directory and add the following code to create a POST endpoint for adding a new user:

```
const express = require('express');
const { Sequelize, DataTypes } = require('sequelize');
require('dotenv').config();

const app = express();
const port = process.env.PORT || 3000;

// Middleware to parse JSON requests
app.use(express.json());

// Connect to PostgreSQL
const sequelize = new Sequelize(process.env.DATABASE_URL, {
    dialect: 'postgres',
    logging: false,
});

// Define User Model
const User = sequelize.define('User', {
    UserID: {
        type: DataTypes.INTEGER,
        autoIncrement: true,
        primaryKey: true,
    },
    UserName: {
        type: DataTypes.STRING,
        allowNull: false,
    },
    Email: {
        type: DataTypes.STRING,
        allowNull: false,
        unique: true,
    },
});
```

```
// Sync the model with the database
sequelize.sync();

// POST endpoint to create a new user
app.post('/users', async (req, res) => {
    const { UserName, Email } = req.body;

    try {
        const newUser = await User.create({ UserName, Email });
        res.status(201).json({ message: 'User created
        successfully', UserID: newUser.UserID });
    } catch (error) {
        console.error('Error creating user:', error);
        if (error.name === 'SequelizeUniqueConstraintError') {
            return res.status(409).json({ error: 'Email already
            exists' });
        }
        res.status(500).json({ error: 'Could not create user' });
    }
});

// Start the server
app.listen(port, () => {
    console.log(`Server is running on http://localhost:${port}`);
});
```

Explanation:

- **Define User Model**: The User model is defined using Sequelize to represent the Users table in your PostgreSQL database.
- **POST Endpoint**: The /users endpoint accepts POST requests to create a new user. It extracts UserName and Email from the request body and attempts to create a new user in the database.
- **Error Handling**: If the email already exists, a 409 conflict response is returned. Other errors result in a 500 server error response.

Testing the POST Endpoint

Now that you have created your first API endpoint, you should test it to ensure it works correctly.

Using Postman to Test the Endpoint

Open Postman: If you haven't already, open Postman.

Create a New Request:

- Set the request type to POST.
- Enter the URL: http://localhost:3000/users.
- In the **Body** tab, select **raw** and set the type to **JSON**. Enter the following JSON data:

```
{
    "UserName": "John Doe",
    "Email": "john.doe@example.com"
}
```

Send the Request: Click the **Send** button.

Check the Response: You should receive a response indicating that the user was created successfully:

```
{
    "message": "User created successfully",
    "UserID": 1
}
```

Verify in PostgreSQL: You can check that the user was added to the Users table by running a simple SELECT query in the PostgreSQL command line:

```
SELECT * FROM Users;
```

Adding Additional Endpoints

After creating the POST endpoint, you may want to add additional endpoints for reading, updating, and deleting users.

Implementing the GET Endpoint

To retrieve user information, add a GET endpoint:

```
// GET endpoint to retrieve a user by UserID
app.get('/users/:UserID', async (req, res) => {
    const { UserID } = req.params;

    try {
        const user = await User.findByPk(UserID);
        if (user) {
            res.status(200).json(user);
        } else {
            res.status(404).json({ error: 'User not found' });
        }
    } catch (error) {
        console.error('Error retrieving user:', error);
        res.status(500).json({ error: 'Could not retrieve user'
        });
    }
});
```

Implementing the PUT Endpoint

For updating user information, add a PUT endpoint:

```
// PUT endpoint to update a user
app.put('/users/:UserID', async (req, res) => {
    const { UserID } = req.params;
    const { UserName, Email } = req.body;

    try {
        const [updated] = await User.update({ UserName, Email }, {
            where: { UserID }
        });
        if (updated) {
```

```
        const updatedUser = await User.findByPk(UserID);
        res.status(200).json({ message: 'User updated
        successfully', user: updatedUser });
    } else {
        res.status(404).json({ error: 'User not found' });
    }
} catch (error) {
    console.error('Error updating user:', error);
    res.status(500).json({ error: 'Could not update user' });
}
});
```

Implementing the DELETE Endpoint

To delete a user, add a DELETE endpoint:

```
// DELETE endpoint to delete a user
app.delete('/users/:UserID', async (req, res) => {
    const { UserID } = req.params;

    try {
        const deleted = await User.destroy({
            where: { UserID }
        });
        if (deleted) {
            res.status(204).send();   // No content returned
        } else {
            res.status(404).json({ error: 'User not found' });
        }
    } catch (error) {
        console.error('Error deleting user:', error);
        res.status(500).json({ error: 'Could not delete user' });
    }
});
```

Testing the Additional Endpoints

You can test the newly created endpoints using Postman, following similar steps as you did for the POST endpoint.

- **GET**: Send a GET request to http://localhost:3000/users/1 (replace 1 with the appropriate UserID) to retrieve user information.
- **PUT**: Send a PUT request to http://localhost:3000/users/1 with a JSON body to update user details.
- **DELETE**: Send a DELETE request to http://localhost:3000/users/1 to remove the user.

You have successfully created your first API endpoints for a RESTful API using PostgreSQL and Express. By implementing endpoints for creating, reading, updating, and deleting users, you have established the core functionality of your API.

In this chapter, you learned how to set up a PostgreSQL database, create a basic server with Express, and define the necessary API endpoints for managing user data. As we continue, we will explore advanced topics such as error handling, input validation, and testing to ensure that your API is robust and secure. These features will further enhance the reliability and usability of your RESTful API.

CRUD Operations with PostgreSQL

CRUD operations—Create, Read, Update, and Delete—are essential for managing data in a PostgreSQL database. In this section, we will delve deeper into each of these operations by implementing them in your RESTful API. We'll use the Users table we previously created, expanding our API functionality to handle all CRUD operations effectively.

Create Operation

The Create operation allows you to add new records to the database. In our API, we already implemented this with a POST endpoint to create a new user.

Recap of the Create Endpoint

Here's a reminder of how the POST endpoint for creating a user looks:

```javascript
app.post('/users', async (req, res) => {
    const { UserName, Email } = req.body;

    try {
        const newUser = await User.create({ UserName, Email });
        res.status(201).json({ message: 'User created
        successfully', UserID: newUser.UserID });
    } catch (error) {
        console.error('Error creating user:', error);
        if (error.name === 'SequelizeUniqueConstraintError') {
            return res.status(409).json({ error: 'Email already
            exists' });
        }
        res.status(500).json({ error: 'Could not create user' });
    }
});
```

This endpoint creates a new user and checks for unique constraints on the email to prevent duplicates.

Read Operation

The Read operation retrieves data from the database. In our API, we need endpoints to fetch user data.

Implementing the GET Endpoint

We can add two GET endpoints: one for retrieving a user by their ID and another for retrieving all users.

Retrieve a User by ID:

```javascript
javascript
Copy code
app.get('/users/:UserID', async (req, res) => {
    const { UserID } = req.params;

    try {
```

```
        const user = await User.findByPk(UserID);
        if (user) {
            res.status(200).json(user);
        } else {
            res.status(404).json({ error: 'User not found' });
        }
    } catch (error) {
        console.error('Error retrieving user:', error);
        res.status(500).json({ error: 'Could not retrieve user'
        });
    }
});
```

Retrieve All Users:

```javascript
javascript
Copy code
app.get('/users', async (req, res) => {
    try {
        const users = await User.findAll();
        res.status(200).json(users);
    } catch (error) {
        console.error('Error retrieving users:', error);
        res.status(500).json({ error: 'Could not retrieve users'
        });
    }
});
```

Update Operation

The Update operation modifies an existing record in the database. We already implemented this with a PUT endpoint.

Recap of the Update Endpoint

Here's how the PUT endpoint for updating user information looks:

```
app.put('/users/:UserID', async (req, res) => {
```

```
    const { UserID } = req.params;
    const { UserName, Email } = req.body;

    try {
        const [updated] = await User.update({ UserName, Email }, {
            where: { UserID }
        });
        if (updated) {
            const updatedUser = await User.findByPk(UserID);
            res.status(200).json({ message: 'User updated
            successfully', user: updatedUser });
        } else {
            res.status(404).json({ error: 'User not found' });
        }
    } catch (error) {
        console.error('Error updating user:', error);
        res.status(500).json({ error: 'Could not update user' });
    }
});
```

This endpoint allows you to update a user's information by UserID.

Delete Operation

The Delete operation removes a record from the database. We already implemented this with a DELETE endpoint.

Recap of the Delete Endpoint

Here's how the DELETE endpoint for removing a user looks:

```
app.delete('/users/:UserID', async (req, res) => {
    const { UserID } = req.params;

    try {
        const deleted = await User.destroy({
            where: { UserID }
        });
        if (deleted) {
```

```
            res.status(204).send();  // No content returned
        } else {
            res.status(404).json({ error: 'User not found' });
        }
    } catch (error) {
        console.error('Error deleting user:', error);
        res.status(500).json({ error: 'Could not delete user' });
    }
});
```

This endpoint allows you to delete a user from the database by their UserID.

Testing CRUD Operations

Now that we have implemented all CRUD operations, it's essential to test them to ensure they work as expected. You can use Postman or a similar tool to perform the following tests:

Testing Create Operation

- Send a POST request to http://localhost:3000/users with a JSON body to create a new user.

Testing Read Operations

- Send a GET request to http://localhost:3000/users/1 (or replace 1 with the appropriate UserID) to retrieve user information.
- Send a GET request to http://localhost:3000/users to retrieve all users.

Testing Update Operation

- Send a PUT request to http://localhost:3000/users/1 with a JSON body to update user details.

Testing Delete Operation

- Send a DELETE request to http://localhost:3000/users/1 to delete the user.

Best Practices for CRUD Operations

To ensure efficient and effective CRUD operations in your PostgreSQL-based API, consider the following best practices:

- **Input Validation**: Always validate incoming data before processing it to prevent errors and maintain data integrity.
- **Error Handling**: Implement robust error handling to manage exceptions and provide meaningful error messages to clients.
- **Consistent Responses**: Maintain a consistent structure for API responses, including success and error responses.
- **Optimize Queries**: Analyze your application's data access patterns and optimize SQL queries to improve performance.
- **Use Transactions**: For operations that involve multiple steps or updates to multiple tables, use transactions to ensure data integrity.

You have successfully implemented CRUD operations in your RESTful API using PostgreSQL. By creating endpoints for creating, reading, updating, and deleting users, you have established the core functionality of your API.

In this chapter, you learned how to set up the CRUD operations for managing user data in PostgreSQL. As we continue through this book, we will explore advanced topics such as error handling, input validation, and testing, ensuring that your API is robust, secure, and scalable. These features will further enhance the reliability and usability of your RESTful API.

Handling Errors and Validations in a RESTful API with PostgreSQL

Handling errors and validating inputs are essential components of building a robust RESTful API. Proper error handling ensures that users receive meaningful feedback when something goes wrong, while input validation helps maintain data integrity and security. This section covers best practices for error handling and input validation in your PostgreSQL-based API.

Importance of Error Handling

Error handling is vital for several reasons:

- **User Experience**: Clear error messages help users understand what went wrong and guide them toward corrective action.
- **Debugging**: Comprehensive error logs assist developers in identifying and resolving issues efficiently.
- **Data Integrity**: By managing errors effectively, you can prevent corrupt or invalid data from being stored in your database.

Common Error Types

When building your API, you may encounter various error types. Common categories include:

- **Client Errors (4xx)**: Indicate that the client made a bad request. Examples include:
- 400 Bad Request: The server cannot process the request due to client-side errors (e.g., invalid input).
- 404 Not Found: The requested resource (e.g., user) does not exist.
- 409 Conflict: There is a conflict with the current state of the resource (e.g., attempting to create a user with an existing email).
- **Server Errors (5xx)**: Indicate that the server failed to fulfill a valid request. Examples include:
- 500 Internal Server Error: An unexpected condition prevented the server from fulfilling the request.

Implementing Error Handling in Express

To implement effective error handling in your Express application, consider the following strategies:

Global Error Handling Middleware

Create a global error-handling middleware to catch errors that occur during request processing. This middleware should be added after your routes:

```
// Global error handling middleware
app.use((err, req, res, next) => {
    console.error(err.message);
    res.status(err.status || 500).json({ error: err.message });
});
```

This middleware captures errors thrown during request handling and responds with an appropriate status code and error message.

Try-Catch Blocks for Asynchronous Operations

For asynchronous operations (e.g., database queries), use try-catch blocks to handle potential errors:

```
app.post('/users', async (req, res, next) => {
    const { UserName, Email } = req.body;

    try {
        const newUser = await User.create({ UserName, Email });
        res.status(201).json({ message: 'User created
        successfully', UserID: newUser.UserID });
    } catch (error) {
        console.error('Error creating user:', error);
        if (error.name === 'SequelizeUniqueConstraintError') {
            return res.status(409).json({ error: 'Email already
            exists' });
        }
        next(error); // Pass the error to the global error handler
    }
});
```

In this example, if a unique constraint is violated when attempting to create a user, a specific error message is returned, and the error is passed to the next middleware.

Input Validation

Input validation is critical to ensure that incoming data adheres to expected formats and constraints. This helps prevent errors and protects against malicious input.

Using a Validation Library

To simplify input validation, consider using a library like Joi or express-validator. Here's how to set up validation using Joi.

Install Joi:

```
npm install joi
```

Define a Validation Schema:

Create a validation schema for user data in a separate file (e.g., validators/userValidator.js):

```
const Joi = require('joi');

const userSchema = Joi.object({
    UserName: Joi.string().min(3).max(50).required(),
    Email: Joi.string().email().required()
});

module.exports = userSchema;
```

Integrate Validation into Your Endpoint:

In your API endpoint, use the validation schema to validate incoming data:

```
const userSchema = require('./validators/userValidator');
```

```
app.post('/users', async (req, res, next) => {
    const { error } = userSchema.validate(req.body);

    if (error) {
        return res.status(400).json({ error:
        error.details[0].message });
    }

    const { UserName, Email } = req.body;

    try {
        const newUser = await User.create({ UserName, Email });
        res.status(201).json({ message: 'User created
        successfully', UserID: newUser.UserID });
    } catch (error) {
        console.error('Error creating user:', error);
        if (error.name === 'SequelizeUniqueConstraintError') {
            return res.status(409).json({ error: 'Email already
            exists' });
        }
        next(error);
    }
});
```

Custom Error Handling Logic

You may want to implement specific logic for known error cases. For example, if a user attempts to create a duplicate entry, handle that case explicitly:

```
app.post('/users', async (req, res, next) => {
    const { error } = userSchema.validate(req.body);

    if (error) {
        return res.status(400).json({ error:
        error.details[0].message });
```

157

```
    }

    const { UserName, Email } = req.body;

    try {
        const newUser = await User.create({ UserName, Email });
        res.status(201).json({ message: 'User created
        successfully', UserID: newUser.UserID });
    } catch (error) {
        console.error('Error creating user:', error);
        if (error.name === 'SequelizeUniqueConstraintError') {
            return res.status(409).json({ error: 'Email already
            exists' });
        }
        next(error); // Pass the error to the global error handler
    }
});
```

Logging Errors

Logging errors is crucial for monitoring and debugging your application. Consider using a logging library like winston to manage logging effectively.

Install Winston:

```
npm install winston
```

Set Up Winston: In your index.js, configure Winston for logging:

```
const winston = require('winston');

const logger = winston.createLogger({
    level: 'info',
    format: winston.format.json(),
    transports: [
        new winston.transports.Console(),
        new winston.transports.File({ filename: 'error.log',
```

```
        level: 'error' })
    ]
});

// Example usage in an error handling middleware
app.use((err, req, res, next) => {
    logger.error(err.message);
    res.status(err.status || 500).json({ error: err.message });
});
```

Handling errors and validating input are crucial for building a robust RESTful API with PostgreSQL. By implementing effective error-handling strategies and validating incoming data, you can ensure that your API operates reliably and securely.

In this chapter, you learned how to set up global error handling in Express, implement input validation using Joi, and manage specific error cases effectively. Additionally, you explored the importance of logging errors for debugging and monitoring purposes.

As we continue through this book, we will delve into advanced topics such as securing your API, implementing authentication and authorization, and optimizing performance to ensure that your application is robust, secure, and scalable. These elements will further enhance the reliability and usability of your RESTful API.

Testing Your API

Testing is a crucial step in the development process of a RESTful API. It ensures that your API behaves as expected, meets user requirements, and functions correctly under various conditions. This section covers various methods for testing your API, including manual testing using tools like Postman and automated testing using frameworks like Mocha and Chai.

Importance of API Testing

- **Functionality Verification**: Testing confirms that each API endpoint works as intended and that the expected data is returned for given inputs.
- **Error Handling**: By simulating various scenarios, you can verify that your API handles errors gracefully and returns appropriate messages.
- **Performance Assessment**: Testing can help identify performance bottlenecks and ensure that your API can handle expected loads.
- **Documentation**: Well-defined tests serve as documentation for the API, illustrating how it is expected to behave in different situations.

Manual Testing with Postman

Postman is a widely used tool for manual API testing. It provides an intuitive interface for sending requests and inspecting responses.

Setting Up Postman

Download and Install Postman: If you haven't already, download Postman from the official website.

Create a New Request:

- Open Postman and click on the "+" button to create a new request.
- Set the request type (GET, POST, PUT, DELETE) based on the endpoint you want to test.
- Enter the URL of your API endpoint (e.g., http://localhost:3000/users).

Testing CRUD Operations

- **Testing Create Operation** (POST):
- Select POST as the request type.
- Enter the URL: http://localhost:3000/users.
- In the Body tab, select raw and choose JSON format. Enter the following JSON data:

```
{
    "UserName": "Alice Johnson",
    "Email": "alice.johnson@example.com"
}
```

- Click **Send** and check the response. You should see a success message similar to:

```
{
    "message": "User created successfully",
    "UserID": 1
}
```

- **Testing Read Operation** (GET):
- Select GET as the request type.
- Enter the URL: http://localhost:3000/users/1 (replace 1 with the appropriate UserID).
- Click **Send** and verify that the correct user data is returned.
- **Testing Update Operation** (PUT):
- Select PUT as the request type.
- Enter the URL: http://localhost:3000/users/1.
- In the Body tab, provide updated JSON data:

```
{
    "UserName": "Alice Smith",
    "Email": "alice.smith@example.com"
}
```

- Click **Send** and check the response for a success message indicating the user was updated.
- **Testing Delete Operation** (DELETE):
- Select DELETE as the request type.
- Enter the URL: http://localhost:3000/users/1.
- Click **Send** and confirm that the response status is 204 (No Content).

Automated Testing with Mocha and Chai

Automated testing is essential for ensuring that your API functions correctly and efficiently. It allows you to run multiple tests quickly and consistently.

3.1 Setting Up Mocha and Chai

1. **Install Mocha and Chai**: In your project directory, install Mocha (the testing framework) and Chai (the assertion library):

```
npm install --save-dev mocha chai chai-http
```

Create a Test Directory: Create a directory for your tests (e.g., test) in your project root.

Create a Test File: Inside the test directory, create a file named users.test.js.

Writing Tests

Here's a basic example of how to write tests for your API using Mocha and Chai:

```
const chai = require('chai');
const chaiHttp = require('chai-http');
const app = require('../src/index'); // Import your Express app
```

```
const expect = chai.expect;

chai.use(chaiHttp);

describe('User API', () => {
    it('should create a new user', (done) => {
        chai.request(app)
            .post('/users')
            .send({ UserName: 'Alice Johnson', Email:
            'alice.johnson@example.com' })
            .end((err, res) => {
                expect(res).to.have.status(201);
                expect(res.body).to.have.property('message',
                'User created successfully');
                expect(res.body).to.have.property('UserID');
                done();
            });
    });

    it('should retrieve a user by ID', (done) => {
        chai.request(app)
            .get('/users/1') // Replace with the appropriate
            UserID
            .end((err, res) => {
                expect(res).to.have.status(200);
                expect(res.body).to.have.property('UserName',
                'Alice Johnson');
                expect(res.body).to.have.property('Email',
                'alice.johnson@example.com');
                done();
            });
    });

    it('should update a user', (done) => {
        chai.request(app)
            .put('/users/1') // Replace with the appropriate
            UserID
            .send({ UserName: 'Alice Smith', Email:
            'alice.smith@example.com' })
            .end((err, res) => {
```

```
                    expect(res).to.have.status(200);
                    expect(res.body).to.have.property('message',
                    'User updated successfully');
                    expect(res.body.user).to.have.property('UserName',
                    'Alice Smith');
                    done();
               });
          });

     it('should delete a user', (done) => {
          chai.request(app)
               .delete('/users/1') // Replace with the appropriate
               UserID
               .end((err, res) => {
                    expect(res).to.have.status(204);
                    done();
               });
          });
     });
});
```

Running the Tests

Modify package.json: Add a test script to your package.json file:

```
"scripts": {
     "test": "mocha"
}
```

Run the Tests: Execute the following command in your terminal:

```
npm test
```

You should see the results of your tests in the terminal, indicating whether they passed or failed.

Best Practices for API Testing

To ensure effective testing of your API, consider the following best practices:

- **Test Coverage**: Aim for comprehensive test coverage that includes all endpoints and various scenarios, including edge cases and error conditions.
- **Use Test Data**: Utilize test data that mimics real-world scenarios. Consider using fixtures or factories to generate consistent test data.
- **Automate Tests**: Automate your tests to save time and ensure consistency. Set up continuous integration (CI) tools to run your tests automatically whenever changes are made.
- **Monitor Performance**: In addition to functional testing, consider performance testing to assess how your API behaves under load. Tools like Apache JMeter or Artillery can help simulate traffic and measure response times.
- **Document Test Cases**: Keep a record of your test cases, including expected inputs and outputs. This documentation can be useful for onboarding new team members and ensuring consistent testing practices.

Testing your API is an essential step in ensuring its reliability and performance. By utilizing tools like Postman for manual testing and frameworks like Mocha and Chai for automated testing, you can ensure that your RESTful API operates as expected and is prepared for real-world usage.

In this chapter, you learned how to set up both manual and automated tests for your CRUD operations, along with best practices for effective API testing. As we progress further in this book, we will explore advanced topics such as securing your API, implementing authentication and authorization, and optimizing performance to ensure that your application is robust, secure, and scalable. These elements will further enhance the reliability and usability of your RESTful API.

Advanced API Features

I mplementing Authentication and Authorization in a RESTful
API
   Authentication and authorization are critical components of
securing your RESTful API. While authentication verifies the identity of
users, authorization determines what those authenticated users are allowed
to do. This chapter will guide you through implementing authentication and
authorization mechanisms in your API using industry-standard practices.

Understanding Authentication and Authorization

- **Authentication**: The process of validating the identity of a user, typically through credentials such as username and password. Successful
  authentication grants the user a token that can be used in subsequent
  requests to identify the user.
- **Authorization**: The process of determining what an authenticated
  user is allowed to do. This can involve permissions based on roles (e.g.,
  admin, user) or specific access rights (e.g., read, write).

Choosing an Authentication Method
Several methods can be used to authenticate users in a RESTful API. The
most common approaches are:

- **Token-Based Authentication**: This method involves issuing a token (often a JSON Web Token, or JWT) to a user upon successful
  authentication. The client sends this token in the HTTP headers for

subsequent requests, allowing the server to verify the user's identity without requiring them to log in repeatedly.

- **Session-Based Authentication**: In this approach, the server creates a session for the user after authentication and stores session information in memory or a database. The client must send a session ID with each request, usually via cookies.

For this chapter, we will focus on implementing **token-based authentication** using JSON Web Tokens (JWT).

Setting Up JWT Authentication
Install Necessary Packages
You will need a few packages to implement JWT authentication. Install the following:

```
npm install jsonwebtoken bcryptjs
```

- **jsonwebtoken**: A library for generating and verifying JSON Web Tokens.
- **bcryptjs**: A library for hashing passwords.

Creating User Registration Endpoint
First, create an endpoint for user registration that hashes passwords before storing them in the database.

```
const bcrypt = require('bcryptjs');

// Registration endpoint
app.post('/register', async (req, res) => {
    const { UserName, Email, Password } = req.body;
```

```
try {
    const hashedPassword = await bcrypt.hash(Password, 10);
    const newUser = await User.create({ UserName, Email,
    Password: hashedPassword });
    res.status(201).json({ message: 'User registered
    successfully', UserID: newUser.UserID });
} catch (error) {
    console.error('Error registering user:', error);
    res.status(500).json({ error: 'Could not register user'
    });
}
});
```

Creating User Login Endpoint

Next, create a login endpoint that verifies user credentials and returns a JWT if authentication is successful.

```
const jwt = require('jsonwebtoken');

// Login endpoint
app.post('/login', async (req, res) => {
    const { Email, Password } = req.body;

    try {
        const user = await User.findOne({ where: { Email } });
        if (!user) {
            return res.status(404).json({ error: 'User not found'
            });
        }

        const isPasswordValid = await bcrypt.compare(Password,
        user.Password);
        if (!isPasswordValid) {
            return res.status(401).json({ error: 'Invalid
            password' });
        }
```

```
        const token = jwt.sign({ UserID: user.UserID, UserName:
        user.UserName }, process.env.JWT_SECRET, {
            expiresIn: '1h',
        });

        res.status(200).json({ message: 'Login successful', token
        });
    } catch (error) {
        console.error('Error logging in user:', error);
        res.status(500).json({ error: 'Could not log in user' });
    }
});
```

Verifying the JWT

To secure your API endpoints, you need a middleware function that
verifies the JWT included in the request headers.

```
const authenticateJWT = (req, res, next) => {
    const token = req.headers['authorization']?.split(' ')[1]; //
    Bearer token format

    if (!token) {
        return res.sendStatus(403); // Forbidden
    }

    jwt.verify(token, process.env.JWT_SECRET, (err, user) => {
        if (err) {
            return res.sendStatus(403); // Forbidden
        }
        req.user = user; // Save the user info for further use
        next();
    });
};
```

Implementing Authorization

With authentication in place, you can now implement authorization based on user roles.

Role-Based Authorization

Assume you have different roles for users (e.g., admin, regular user). You can add a role column to your Users table:

```
ALTER TABLE Users ADD COLUMN role VARCHAR(20) DEFAULT 'user';
```

Middleware for Role Checking

Create a middleware function to check if a user has the appropriate role to access a specific endpoint.

```
const authorizeRole = (roles) => {
    return (req, res, next) => {
        if (!req.user || !roles.includes(req.user.role)) {
            return res.status(403).json({ error: 'Access denied'
            });
        }
        next();
    };
};
```

Protecting Endpoints with Authorization

You can now protect your endpoints using the authenticateJWT and authorizeRole middleware.

```
app.get('/admin', authenticateJWT, authorizeRole(['admin']),
(req, res) => {
    res.status(200).json({ message: 'Welcome, admin!' });
});
```

Testing Authentication and Authorization

After implementing authentication and authorization, it's essential to test these features thoroughly.

Testing User Registration and Login

Register a User: Send a POST request to /register with a JSON body containing user details.

Log In: Send a POST request to /login with the user's email and password. Ensure you receive a JWT in the response.

Testing Protected Endpoints

Access a Protected Endpoint: Send a GET request to /admin without a token to check for access denial.

Access with Token: Include the JWT in the Authorization header (as a Bearer token) and verify that you gain access to the protected endpoint.

Best Practices for Implementing Authentication and Authorization

- **Use HTTPS**: Always use HTTPS to secure data transmission, especially when handling authentication credentials.
- **Limit Token Lifetime**: Use short-lived tokens (e.g., 1 hour) and implement refresh tokens to enhance security.
- **Store Secrets Securely**: Use environment variables to store sensitive information like your JWT secret.
- **Rate Limiting**: Implement rate limiting to prevent abuse of your login endpoint.
- **Log Authentication Attempts**: Keep logs of successful and failed authentication attempts for auditing and monitoring purposes.

In this chapter, you learned how to implement authentication and authorization in your RESTful API using JSON Web Tokens (JWT) and role-based access control. By following best practices and utilizing secure coding techniques, you can protect your API from unauthorized access and ensure that only authenticated users can perform actions based on their roles.

As we progress further in this book, we will explore additional advanced features such as API versioning, pagination, and optimizing performance, which will further enhance the functionality and security of your RESTful

API.

Pagination and Filtering in a RESTful API

Pagination and filtering are essential features for improving the performance and usability of your RESTful API, especially when dealing with large datasets. These techniques allow clients to retrieve only the data they need, reducing the amount of data transferred over the network and improving response times. This section will explore how to implement pagination and filtering in your API using PostgreSQL.

Importance of Pagination and Filtering

- **Performance Optimization**: By limiting the amount of data sent in a single request, pagination helps reduce server load and response times.
- **Improved User Experience**: Pagination allows users to navigate through large datasets easily, providing a more user-friendly experience.
- **Efficient Data Retrieval**: Filtering helps clients retrieve only relevant data, minimizing unnecessary processing and improving efficiency.

Implementing Pagination

2.1 Understanding Pagination Concepts

Pagination is typically implemented using two main parameters: **limit** and **offset**.

- **Limit**: Specifies the maximum number of records to return in a single response.
- **Offset**: Specifies the number of records to skip before starting to return records.

For example, if you want to return 10 users starting from the 21st user, you would set limit to 10 and offset to 20.

Adding Pagination to Your API Endpoint

To implement pagination for the endpoint that retrieves all users, modify the GET /users endpoint to accept limit and offset parameters.

```
app.get('/users', async (req, res) => {
    const limit = parseInt(req.query.limit) || 10; // Default
    limit to 10
    const offset = parseInt(req.query.offset) || 0; // Default
    offset to 0

    try {
        const users = await User.findAll({
            limit,
            offset,
        });
        res.status(200).json(users);
    } catch (error) {
        console.error('Error retrieving users:', error);
        res.status(500).json({ error: 'Could not retrieve users'
        });
    }
});
```

Testing Pagination

To test pagination, you can use Postman or a similar tool:

Test with Default Values: Send a GET request to http://localhost:3000/users to retrieve the first 10 users.

Test with Parameters: Send a GET request to http://localhost:3000/users?limit=5&offset=10 to retrieve 5 users starting from the 11th user.

Implementing Filtering

Understanding Filtering Concepts

Filtering allows clients to specify criteria for which records to retrieve. This can include filtering based on specific fields (e.g., UserName, Email) and can be combined with pagination.

Adding Filtering to Your API Endpoint

You can implement filtering in the same GET /users endpoint by adding query parameters for the fields you want to filter. For example, you might want to filter users by their UserName or Email.

```
app.get('/users', async (req, res) => {
    const limit = parseInt(req.query.limit) || 10;
    const offset = parseInt(req.query.offset) || 0;
    const { UserName, Email } = req.query;

    const whereClause = {};
    if (UserName) {
        whereClause.UserName = { [Op.iLike]: `%${UserName}%` };
        // Case-insensitive like query
    }
    if (Email) {
        whereClause.Email = { [Op.iLike]: `%${Email}%` };
    }

    try {
        const users = await User.findAll({
            where: whereClause,
            limit,
            offset,
        });
        res.status(200).json(users);
    } catch (error) {
        console.error('Error retrieving users:', error);
        res.status(500).json({ error: 'Could not retrieve users'
        });
    }
});
```

Testing Filtering

To test filtering:

Filter by UserName: Send a GET request to http://localhost:3000/user s?UserName=Alice to retrieve users whose UserName contains "Alice".

Filter by Email: Send a GET request to http://localhost:3000/us ers?Email=john@example.com to retrieve users whose Email matches "john@example.com".

Combine Filtering and Pagination: Send a GET request to http://local host:3000/users?UserName=Alice&limit=5&offset=0 to retrieve the first 5 users whose UserName contains "Alice".

Best Practices for Pagination and Filtering

To ensure effective implementation of pagination and filtering, consider the following best practices:

- **Default Values**: Always provide sensible default values for pagination parameters (e.g., limit) to prevent overwhelming the server with large requests.
- **Input Validation**: Validate query parameters to ensure they meet expected formats and types, providing feedback for invalid inputs.
- **Performance Considerations**: Monitor and optimize database queries, especially with large datasets. Consider using indexes on frequently filtered columns to improve query performance.
- **Clear Documentation**: Document the available query parameters for pagination and filtering in your API documentation to inform users how to use these features effectively.
- **Response Metadata**: Consider including metadata in your response to inform clients about the total number of records, current page, and total pages available. This helps clients manage pagination more effectively.

Implementing pagination and filtering in your RESTful API enhances its performance and usability, allowing clients to retrieve only the data they need efficiently. By providing clear options for limiting and filtering data, you can significantly improve the user experience while optimizing server load.

In this chapter, you learned how to add pagination and filtering capabilities to your API endpoints. As we continue through this book, we will explore additional advanced features, such as search functionality, sorting, and optimizing database queries, ensuring that your API is both powerful and efficient.

Versioning Your API

API versioning is a critical practice that allows developers to manage changes and enhancements to their API while maintaining compatibility with existing clients. As your application evolves, new features, improvements, or changes may necessitate breaking changes that could disrupt existing integrations. This chapter will discuss the importance of API versioning, different strategies for versioning, and best practices for implementing it in your RESTful API.

Importance of API Versioning

- **Backward Compatibility**: Versioning allows you to introduce new features or changes without breaking existing clients that rely on earlier versions of the API.
- **Ease of Maintenance**: Different versions can coexist, making it easier to maintain and support multiple client applications simultaneously.
- **Client Flexibility**: Clients can choose when to upgrade to newer versions, giving them control over their integration and reducing potential disruptions.

Strategies for API Versioning

There are several common strategies for versioning APIs. Each approach has its advantages and disadvantages, and the best choice depends on your specific use case and requirements.

URI Versioning

This is one of the most common and straightforward methods of versioning APIs. In this approach, the version number is included in the URL path.

- **Example**:

```
GET /v1/users
GET /v2/users
```

Advantages:

- Simple to implement and understand.
- Clear separation of versions in the API URL.

Disadvantages:

- Can lead to URL bloat if multiple versions are maintained long-term.
- Requires clients to update their integration with new URLs.

Query Parameter Versioning

In this approach, the version number is specified as a query parameter in the API request.

- **Example**:

```
GET /users?version=1
GET /users?version=2
```

Advantages:

- Easy to implement without changing the base URL.
- Clients can easily switch versions without modifying the URL structure.

Disadvantages:

- The version is less visible compared to URI versioning.

- May complicate caching mechanisms.

Header Versioning

With header versioning, the version information is included in the request headers instead of the URL.

- **Example**:

```
GET /users
Headers:
{
    "Accept": "application/vnd.myapi.v1+json"
}
```

Advantages:

- Keeps the URL clean and unchanged.
- Allows for more flexibility in defining content negotiation.

Disadvantages:

- Version information is not visible in the URL, making it harder for clients to discover available versions.
- Clients may need to be familiar with using headers.

Content Negotiation Versioning

This approach involves using the Accept header to specify the desired version of the response.

- **Example**:

```
GET /users
Headers:
{
    "Accept": "application/json; version=1"
}
```

Advantages:

- Provides a clean URL structure.
- Allows clients to request different versions based on content types.

Disadvantages:

- Requires additional implementation effort to handle content negotiation.
- Less intuitive for clients who may not be familiar with this method.

Implementing Versioning in Your API

For this example, we will implement **URI versioning** for our RESTful API using Express.

Structuring Your Routes

You can structure your API routes to include versioning. For instance:

```
// V1 Routes
app.use('/api/v1/users', userRoutesV1);

// V2 Routes
app.use('/api/v2/users', userRoutesV2);
```

Each version can have its own set of route handlers. For example, you might have different logic for the user endpoints in version 1 and version 2.

Creating Route Files

Create Directories for Versioned Routes: Create directories for your versioned routes, such as src/routes/v1 and src/routes/v2.

Implement Route Logic:

For v1 (src/routes/v1/users.js):

```
const express = require('express');
const router = express.Router();

// Define version 1 user routes
router.get('/', async (req, res) => {
    // Logic for getting users in version 1
    res.json({ message: 'List of users in version 1' });
});

module.exports = router;
```

For v2 (src/routes/v2/users.js):

```
const express = require('express');
const router = express.Router();

// Define version 2 user routes
router.get('/', async (req, res) => {
    // Logic for getting users in version 2
    res.json({ message: 'List of users in version 2 with more
    features' });
});

module.exports = router;
```

Updating Your Main Application File

In your main index.js file, ensure you include the versioned routes:

```
const express = require('express');
```

```
const userRoutesV1 = require('./routes/v1/users');
const userRoutesV2 = require('./routes/v2/users');

const app = express();

// Middleware and other configurations...

// Use versioned routes
app.use('/api/v1/users', userRoutesV1);
app.use('/api/v2/users', userRoutesV2);

// Start the server
app.listen(port, () => {
    console.log(`Server is running on http://localhost:${port}`);
});
```

Best Practices for API Versioning

To implement effective API versioning, consider the following best practices:

- **Document Changes**: Clearly document changes between versions in your API documentation. Include details about deprecated features and any breaking changes.
- **Maintain Old Versions**: If possible, maintain support for older versions of the API for a reasonable time to allow clients to transition to newer versions smoothly.
- **Use Semantic Versioning**: Consider using semantic versioning principles (major.minor.patch) to communicate the significance of changes in your API.
- **Notify Clients of Changes**: When you release a new version, notify clients through release notes or communication channels, giving them time to adjust.
- **Plan for Deprecation**: Establish a clear deprecation policy that outlines how long old versions will be supported and how clients will be notified of upcoming deprecations.

API versioning is a critical aspect of managing your RESTful API, allowing you to introduce changes and improvements without disrupting existing clients. By employing strategies such as URI versioning, you can maintain backward compatibility while evolving your API to meet new requirements.

In this chapter, you learned about different versioning strategies, how to implement URI versioning in your API, and best practices for managing API versions. As we move forward, we will explore additional advanced features such as caching, rate limiting, and securing your API, which will enhance the performance and security of your RESTful API.

Performance Optimization Techniques

Optimizing Queries in DynamoDB
    DynamoDB is a fully managed NoSQL database service that provides high performance at scale. However, to fully leverage its capabilities, it is essential to optimize your queries for speed, efficiency, and cost-effectiveness. This chapter will cover various techniques for optimizing queries in DynamoDB, including data modeling strategies, effective use of indexes, query patterns, and performance best practices.

Understanding DynamoDB Query Basics

In DynamoDB, data is organized into tables, and queries are made primarily through two operations: **GetItem** and **Query**. Understanding how these operations work is crucial for optimizing query performance.

- **GetItem**: Retrieves a single item from a table by its primary key. It is the most efficient way to fetch data and incurs minimal latency.
- **Query**: Retrieves multiple items from a table based on a primary key or a secondary index. Query operations are efficient but can be affected by how the data is modeled and indexed.

Data Modeling for Performance
Use Composite Primary Keys

DynamoDB supports two types of primary keys: simple primary keys (partition key only) and composite primary keys (partition key and sort key). Using composite primary keys can significantly enhance your query performance by allowing you to query items that share the same partition key while also sorting by the sort key.

Example:

```
Partition Key: UserID
Sort Key: Timestamp
```

This setup allows you to query all activities for a user and sort them by timestamp, which is efficient for time-based queries.

Denormalization

DynamoDB encourages a denormalized data model where data is duplicated across items to reduce the need for complex joins. This can lead to more efficient read operations.

Example: Instead of having separate tables for user profiles and user activity, you can store activity data directly within the user profile item or use a single table with a composite key structure.

Choosing the Right Partition Key

Selecting an appropriate partition key is crucial for evenly distributing data across partitions. A good partition key should have high cardinality and ensure that writes are evenly distributed.

Example: Instead of using UserID as a partition key, you might consider adding a hash prefix based on user attributes, such as UserType#UserID, to increase distribution across partitions.

Effective Use of Indexes

Indexes play a significant role in optimizing query performance in DynamoDB. They allow for efficient lookups and can improve read performance without needing to scan the entire table.

Global Secondary Indexes (GSIs)

GSIs allow you to create alternative query patterns for your data without affecting the primary key. They consist of an index partition key and an optional sort key, enabling you to query the data differently.

Example: If your primary access pattern is by UserID, but you also frequently query by Email, you can create a GSI with Email as the partition key.

Local Secondary Indexes (LSIs)

LSIs enable you to create alternative sort keys for items sharing the same partition key. This is useful for queries that require sorting or filtering on different attributes.

Example: If you have a composite primary key of UserID and Timestamp, but you also want to sort by ActivityType, you can create an LSI with ActivityType as the sort key.

Optimizing Query Patterns

Use Query Instead of Scan

DynamoDB scans read every item in the table and can be costly in terms of read capacity units (RCUs). Instead, use the Query operation whenever possible, as it retrieves items based on specific keys and is more efficient.

Filtering Results

You can use filter expressions to narrow down results after a query. However, filtering results does not reduce the read capacity units consumed, so it's better to design your table to minimize the need for filters.

Example: Instead of querying for all items and filtering out unwanted results, structure your data model to include attributes that allow for more specific queries.

Limit the Number of Returned Attributes

When querying, specify only the attributes you need using the Projection-Expression parameter. This reduces the amount of data transferred over the network and can improve performance.

Example:

```
const params = {
    TableName: 'Users',
    KeyConditionExpression: 'UserID = :uid',
```

```
ProjectionExpression: 'UserName, Email',
ExpressionAttributeValues: {
    ':uid': '123',
},
};
```

Monitoring and Performance Best Practices

Use DynamoDB Metrics and CloudWatch

Utilize Amazon CloudWatch to monitor DynamoDB performance metrics, such as read and write capacity usage, throttling events, and latency. This data can help identify bottlenecks and inform your optimization strategies.

Optimize Capacity Settings

DynamoDB offers both on-demand and provisioned capacity modes. For applications with unpredictable workloads, consider using on-demand capacity to automatically scale based on traffic. For predictable workloads, provisioned capacity allows you to set specific limits and can be more cost-effective.

Enable DynamoDB Accelerator (DAX)

DAX is an in-memory caching service for DynamoDB that can significantly improve read performance by reducing latency. It's especially useful for applications requiring microsecond response times for read-heavy workloads.

Implementing Backoff and Retry Logic

When throttling occurs (due to exceeding provisioned throughput), implement exponential backoff and retry logic in your application to manage the load more effectively and avoid overwhelming the database.

Optimizing queries in DynamoDB is essential for achieving high performance and cost-efficiency. By employing effective data modeling strategies, utilizing indexes appropriately, and optimizing query patterns, you can significantly enhance the performance of your RESTful API.

Optimizing Queries in PostgreSQL

PostgreSQL is a powerful, open-source relational database that provides robust performance and extensive features. However, as data volumes grow and queries become more complex, optimizing query performance becomes essential. This chapter will explore various techniques for optimizing queries in PostgreSQL, including indexing strategies, query design best practices, and monitoring tools.

Understanding Query Performance

Query Execution Plan

PostgreSQL uses a query execution plan to determine the most efficient way to execute a query. You can use the EXPLAIN statement to view the execution plan, which provides insights into how the query will be processed.

```
EXPLAIN SELECT * FROM users WHERE UserID = 1;
```

This command returns information about the query plan, including the estimated cost, number of rows processed, and the method used (e.g., Sequential Scan, Index Scan).

Indexing Strategies

Indexes are critical for optimizing query performance in PostgreSQL. They allow the database to find rows more quickly, especially in large tables.

Choosing the Right Index Type

PostgreSQL supports several index types, each suitable for different use cases:

- **B-tree Index**: The default and most common index type. Suitable for equality and range queries.

```
CREATE INDEX idx_users_email ON users (Email);
```

- **Hash Index**: Suitable for equality comparisons. Note that hash indexes are less commonly used due to their limitations in PostgreSQL versions prior to 10.

```
CREATE INDEX idx_users_hash ON users USING HASH (UserID);
```

- **GIN (Generalized Inverted Index)**: Useful for indexing composite data types like arrays or JSONB. Ideal for full-text search.

```
CREATE INDEX idx_users_tags ON users USING GIN (tags);
```

- **GiST (Generalized Search Tree)**: Useful for geometric data types and full-text search.

```
CREATE INDEX idx_users_location ON users USING GiST (location);
```

Multi-Column Indexes

Creating indexes on multiple columns can significantly improve performance for queries that filter or sort on multiple attributes.

```
CREATE INDEX idx_users_name_email ON users (UserName, Email);
```

This index is beneficial for queries that filter or sort using both UserName and Email.

Index Maintenance

- Regularly monitor and maintain your indexes. Use the REINDEX command to rebuild corrupted indexes and VACUUM to reclaim storage.

```
VACUUM ANALYZE users;
```

This command updates statistics used by the query planner, improving the accuracy of the execution plan.

Query Design Best Practices
Write Efficient Queries

- **Select Only Needed Columns**: Avoid SELECT *. Specify only the columns you need to reduce data transfer and processing time.

```
SELECT UserName, Email FROM users WHERE UserID = 1;
```

- **Use WHERE Clauses Effectively**: Filter results as early as possible to reduce the number of rows processed.

```
SELECT * FROM users WHERE Active = true;
```

Joins Optimization

- **Use Proper Join Types**: Choose the appropriate join type (INNER, LEFT, RIGHT) based on your requirements. Avoid unnecessary joins to reduce complexity.
- **Ensure Join Conditions are Indexed**: If you're joining on foreign keys, ensure those keys are indexed to speed up join operations.

Avoid Subqueries When Possible

- Use joins instead of subqueries for better performance. Subqueries can sometimes lead to less efficient execution plans.

```
-- Instead of:
SELECT * FROM users WHERE UserID IN (SELECT UserID FROM orders);

-- Use:
SELECT u.* FROM users u JOIN orders o ON u.UserID = o.UserID;
```

Monitoring and Performance Tuning
Using PostgreSQL Logs

Enable query logging in PostgreSQL to monitor slow queries. You can adjust settings in postgresql.conf:

```
log_min_duration_statement = 1000  # Log queries taking longer
than 1 second
```

After adjusting the settings, restart the PostgreSQL server. Analyze the logs to identify and optimize slow-performing queries.

pg_stat_statements

The pg_stat_statements extension provides insights into the performance of your SQL statements, including execution counts and average time taken. Enable it by modifying your postgresql.conf:

```
shared_preload_libraries = 'pg_stat_statements'
```

After restarting, create the extension:

```
CREATE EXTENSION pg_stat_statements;
```

You can now query the pg_stat_statements view to find slow or frequently executed queries:

```
SELECT * FROM pg_stat_statements ORDER BY total_time DESC LIMIT
10;
```

Analyze and Vacuum

Regularly run the ANALYZE command to update statistics used by the query planner, and VACUUM to reclaim storage:

```
ANALYZE users;
VACUUM users;
```

Caching Strategies

Use Connection Pooling

Implement connection pooling to manage database connections efficiently, especially in applications with high concurrency. Libraries like pg-pool can help manage connections effectively.

Implement Query Caching

For frequently executed queries, consider implementing a caching layer (e.g., Redis) to store query results temporarily. This reduces the load on the database and speeds up response times for repeated queries.

Optimizing queries in PostgreSQL is vital for achieving high performance and efficiency in your applications. By employing effective indexing strategies, writing efficient queries, and utilizing monitoring tools, you can significantly enhance the performance of your RESTful API.

Caching Strategies for Improved Performance

Caching is an essential technique for enhancing the performance of your RESTful API. By storing frequently accessed data in a cache, you can reduce database load, decrease latency, and improve response times for users. This chapter will discuss various caching strategies, their benefits, and implementation techniques for your API.

Understanding Caching

Caching involves storing copies of files or data in a cache (temporary storage) so that future requests for that data can be served faster. Caching is particularly useful for data that is expensive to fetch or compute, such as:

- Frequently accessed database queries.
- API responses that don't change often.
- Computed results from complex calculations.

Benefits of Caching

- **Reduced Latency**: Cached data can be retrieved more quickly than data fetched from a database, leading to faster response times.
- **Lower Database Load**: By serving cached data, you reduce the number

of read operations against your database, which can decrease costs and improve overall system performance.

- **Scalability**: Caching helps your application handle more requests simultaneously without overwhelming the database.

Caching Strategies

Several caching strategies can be implemented, each suitable for different use cases:

3.1 In-Memory Caching

In-memory caching stores data in the memory (RAM) of the server for ultra-fast access. Common libraries and systems include:

- **Redis**: An in-memory data structure store that supports various data types, including strings, hashes, and lists. It is widely used for caching due to its speed and flexibility.
- **Memcached**: A memory-caching system designed for simplicity and performance. It is suitable for caching small objects.

Example of Using Redis:

Install Redis: If Redis is not already installed, you can download and install it from the Redis website.

Integrate Redis with Your API:

Install the Redis client for Node.js:

```
npm install redis
```

Set Up Redis Client: In your application, set up a Redis client to interact with the cache.

```
const redis = require('redis');
```

```
const client = redis.createClient();

client.on('error', (err) => {
    console.error('Redis error:', err);
});
```

Cache Data: When querying the database, first check if the data exists in the cache before querying the database.

```
app.get('/users/:id', async (req, res) => {
    const { id } = req.params;

    // Check cache for user data
    client.get(`user:${id}`, async (err, result) => {
        if (err) throw err;

        if (result) {
            // Return cached data
            return res.status(200).json(JSON.parse(result));
        } else {
            // Query the database
            const user = await User.findByPk(id);
            if (user) {
                // Store the result in cache
                client.setex(`user:${id}`, 3600,
                JSON.stringify(user)); // Cache for 1 hour
                return res.status(200).json(user);
            } else {
                return res.status(404).json({ error: 'User not
                found' });
            }
        }
    });
});
```

HTTP Caching

HTTP caching leverages browser and intermediary caches to reduce server load and latency. You can control caching behavior using HTTP headers.

- **Cache-Control**: Specifies directives for caching mechanisms in both requests and responses.
- **ETag**: A unique identifier for a specific version of a resource. If the resource changes, a new ETag is generated.
- **Last-Modified**: Indicates the last time the resource was modified.

Example of Setting Caching Headers:

```
app.get('/users', (req, res) => {
    res.set('Cache-Control', 'public, max-age=3600'); // Cache
    for 1 hour
    res.json(users);
});
```

Application-Level Caching

This strategy involves caching data at the application level, which is useful for caching computed results, temporary data, or session information.

- **In-memory objects**: Store data in memory using variables or data structures within your application.
- **File-based caching**: Write cached data to files on disk, allowing for persistence between server restarts.

Example of In-Memory Caching:

```
const userCache = {}; // Simple in-memory cache

app.get('/users/:id', async (req, res) => {
    const { id } = req.params;
```

```
if (userCache[id]) {
    return res.status(200).json(userCache[id]); // Return
    cached user data
}

const user = await User.findByPk(id);
if (user) {
    userCache[id] = user; // Store user in cache
    return res.status(200).json(user);
} else {
    return res.status(404).json({ error: 'User not found' });
}
});
```

Best Practices for Caching

To maximize the effectiveness of your caching strategy, consider the following best practices:

- **Cache Invalidation**: Implement strategies for invalidating or refreshing cached data when the underlying data changes. This can include time-based expiration, explicit invalidation on data updates, or versioning.
- **Data Expiration**: Set appropriate expiration times for cached data to ensure that stale data is not served to users. Use the setex method in Redis to set an expiration time.
- **Monitor Cache Performance**: Regularly monitor your cache hit and miss rates. High hit rates indicate that your caching strategy is effective, while high miss rates may suggest a need for adjustment.
- **Use Appropriate Cache Keys**: Design cache keys that uniquely identify cached data and avoid collisions. Include relevant parameters, such as user IDs or query parameters.
- **Avoid Over-Caching**: While caching is beneficial, over-caching can lead to increased complexity and stale data. Cache only data that provides a significant performance benefit.

Caching is a powerful technique that can significantly enhance the performance of your RESTful API. By implementing effective caching strategies such as in-memory caching, HTTP caching, and application-level caching, you can reduce latency, lower database load, and improve the overall user experience.

Monitoring and Troubleshooting Performance Issues

Effective monitoring and troubleshooting are essential components of maintaining a high-performance RESTful API. By actively tracking performance metrics, diagnosing issues, and implementing corrective measures, you can ensure that your API remains responsive and reliable. This chapter will explore various monitoring tools, techniques for diagnosing performance issues, and best practices for troubleshooting.

Importance of Monitoring

Monitoring is vital for understanding the health and performance of your API. It allows you to:

- **Detect Performance Bottlenecks**: Identify slow requests, high latency, and resource constraints before they impact users.
- **Track Usage Patterns**: Understand how users interact with your API, helping to inform optimization strategies and capacity planning.
- **Ensure Reliability**: Monitor for errors and downtime to maintain the overall reliability of your service.

Key Performance Metrics to Monitor

When monitoring your RESTful API, focus on the following key performance metrics:

- **Response Time**: Measure the time it takes for the server to respond to a request. This is critical for user experience and can indicate

197

performance issues.

- **Error Rate**: Track the percentage of failed requests compared to total requests. A sudden spike in errors may indicate underlying issues.
- **Throughput**: Measure the number of requests processed per second. This helps assess how well your API handles increased load.
- **Resource Utilization**: Monitor CPU, memory, and disk usage on your server. High resource utilization can lead to degraded performance and may require scaling or optimization.
- **Database Performance**: Keep an eye on database query performance, including slow queries and lock contention. Tools like pg_stat_statements in PostgreSQL can provide insights into query performance.

Monitoring Tools

Several tools and services can help you monitor your API effectively:

Application Performance Monitoring (APM) Tools

APM tools provide insights into application performance by tracking metrics, errors, and transaction traces. Popular APM tools include:

- **New Relic**: Offers performance monitoring, error tracking, and detailed transaction analysis.
- **Datadog**: Provides real-time monitoring, dashboards, and alerts for applications and infrastructure.
- **Dynatrace**: Uses AI to monitor application performance and user experience, providing deep insights.

Logging Solutions

Implement structured logging to capture essential data about requests, responses, errors, and performance. Some popular logging libraries and services include:

- **Winston**: A versatile logging library for Node.js that supports multiple transports (console, file, etc.).
- **Loggly**: A cloud-based log management solution that provides search-

ing, filtering, and alerting.

- **Elastic Stack (ELK)**: Comprising Elasticsearch, Logstash, and Kibana, the ELK stack offers powerful logging, searching, and visualization capabilities.

Monitoring Database Performance

For database monitoring, consider using tools that specialize in tracking performance metrics:

- **pgAdmin**: A popular PostgreSQL management tool that includes monitoring features.
- **pg_stat_statements**: An extension that tracks execution statistics of SQL statements.
- **AWS CloudWatch**: If you're using Amazon RDS for PostgreSQL, CloudWatch provides metrics for database performance.

Diagnosing Performance Issues

When performance issues arise, it's crucial to diagnose the root cause effectively. Consider the following steps:

Analyze Logs

Review application logs for error messages, stack traces, and performance metrics. Look for patterns or anomalies that may indicate issues.

Use APM Insights

Utilize APM tools to identify slow transactions and the specific components (e.g., database queries, external API calls) contributing to latency.

Check Database Performance

Use PostgreSQL monitoring tools to check for slow queries, locks, and overall database performance. The EXPLAIN command can help analyze the execution plans of slow queries.

```
EXPLAIN ANALYZE SELECT * FROM users WHERE Email =
```

```
'test@example.com';
```

Conduct Load Testing

Simulate traffic to your API to understand how it performs under different loads. Tools like Apache JMeter, Gatling, and Artillery can help assess your API's capacity and identify breaking points.

Troubleshooting Common Performance Issues
Slow Queries

- **Solution**: Analyze and optimize slow queries using indexing, query refactoring, and caching strategies.

High Error Rates

- **Solution**: Investigate the underlying causes of errors, such as input validation issues, database timeouts, or service dependencies. Implement proper error handling and logging.

High Latency

- **Solution**: Check for network issues, database performance, and server resource utilization. Optimize your API endpoints to reduce response times.

Resource Exhaustion

- **Solution**: Monitor resource utilization metrics. If your application is reaching its resource limits, consider scaling your infrastructure (vertical or horizontal scaling) or optimizing resource usage.

Best Practices for Monitoring and Troubleshooting

- **Set Up Alerts**: Use monitoring tools to set up alerts for critical performance metrics (e.g., response time, error rate). This helps you respond to issues proactively.
- **Establish Baselines**: Track performance metrics over time to establish normal baselines. This will help you identify anomalies and trends.
- **Regularly Review Logs**: Schedule regular log reviews to catch issues early. Automated log analysis can help highlight significant patterns or errors.
- **Optimize Continuously**: Performance optimization is an ongoing process. Regularly revisit and refine your application and database performance based on monitoring data and user feedback.

Monitoring and troubleshooting performance issues are crucial for maintaining a responsive and reliable RESTful API. By actively tracking key performance metrics, utilizing monitoring tools, and implementing best practices for diagnosis and troubleshooting, you can ensure that your API meets user expectations and handles increased load effectively.

Security Considerations

Securing RESTful APIs

As APIs become integral to modern applications, securing them is paramount. A compromised API can lead to unauthorized access, data breaches, and severe reputational damage. This chapter will explore best practices for securing RESTful APIs, including authentication, authorization, encryption, and input validation, among other strategies.

Understanding API Security Risks

APIs face various security risks, including:

- **Unauthorized Access**: Attackers may exploit vulnerabilities to gain unauthorized access to sensitive data or functions.
- **Data Breaches**: Sensitive information can be exposed if proper security measures are not in place.
- **Denial of Service (DoS)**: Malicious actors may overwhelm an API with traffic, rendering it unusable for legitimate users.
- **Injection Attacks**: APIs are susceptible to SQL injection and other injection attacks if input validation is inadequate.

Understanding these risks is the first step toward implementing robust security measures.

Authentication

Authentication verifies the identity of users or systems attempting to access your API. Effective authentication mechanisms help prevent unauthorized access.

Token-Based Authentication

Token-based authentication, particularly using JSON Web Tokens (JWT), is a common method for securing APIs. Upon successful login, the server issues a token that clients include in subsequent requests.

- **Advantages**:
- Stateless: The server does not need to maintain session state.
- Scalable: Easily scalable for distributed systems.

Multi-Factor Authentication (MFA)

MFA adds an additional layer of security by requiring users to provide two or more verification factors (e.g., something they know, have, or are) before gaining access.

- **Implementation**: Consider using libraries or services (like Authy or Google Authenticator) that support MFA.

Authorization

Authorization determines what authenticated users are allowed to do. Properly implemented authorization mechanisms help restrict access to sensitive resources and operations.

Role-Based Access Control (RBAC)

RBAC assigns permissions based on user roles. This simplifies permission management by grouping permissions for specific roles (e.g., admin, user).

- **Implementation**: Define roles and their associated permissions within your API. Use middleware to enforce role checks.

```
const authorizeRole = (roles) => {
    return (req, res, next) => {
        if (!req.user || !roles.includes(req.user.role)) {
```

```
        return res.status(403).json({ error: 'Access denied'
        });
    }
    next();
    };
};

// Protect a route
app.get('/admin', authenticateJWT, authorizeRole(['admin']),
(req, res) => {
    res.status(200).json({ message: 'Welcome, admin!' });
});
```

Attribute-Based Access Control (ABAC)

ABAC grants permissions based on attributes of the user, resource, and environment. This allows for fine-grained access control.

- **Implementation**: Define policies that evaluate user and resource attributes to determine access permissions.

Data Encryption

Data encryption is crucial for protecting sensitive information both in transit and at rest.

Encryption in Transit

Use HTTPS (HTTP Secure) to encrypt data transmitted between clients and the server. This protects against eavesdropping and man-in-the-middle attacks.

- **Implementation**: Obtain an SSL/TLS certificate and configure your web server (e.g., Nginx, Apache) to enforce HTTPS.

Encryption at Rest

Encrypt sensitive data stored in your database to protect it from unauthorized access.

- **Implementation**: Use database encryption features or encrypt sensitive fields manually using libraries (e.g., crypto in Node.js).

Input Validation

Input validation is essential for preventing injection attacks and ensuring data integrity. Always validate and sanitize user input before processing it.

Validate Input Data

Implement strict validation rules for all incoming data, checking for data type, length, format, and required fields.

- **Implementation**: Use validation libraries like Joi or express-validator to enforce validation rules.

```
const Joi = require('joi');

const userSchema = Joi.object({
    UserName: Joi.string().min(3).max(50).required(),
    Email: Joi.string().email().required(),
});

// Validate incoming request
app.post('/users', (req, res) => {
    const { error } = userSchema.validate(req.body);
    if (error) {
        return res.status(400).json({ error:
        error.details[0].message });
    }
    // Proceed with user creation...
}); Sanitize Input
```

Sanitize input data to remove any potentially harmful content before processing it. This helps mitigate risks from injection attacks.

- **Implementation**: Use libraries like DOMPurify (for web applications) or built-in sanitation functions provided by your framework.

Rate Limiting

Rate limiting controls the number of requests a client can make to your API in a specified time frame. This helps prevent abuse and mitigates DoS attacks.

Implementing Rate Limiting

You can use middleware to implement rate limiting in your API.

- **Implementation**: Use libraries like express-rate-limit to define rate limiting rules.

```
const rateLimit = require('express-rate-limit');

const limiter = rateLimit({
    windowMs: 15 * 60 * 1000, // 15 minutes
    max: 100, // Limit each IP to 100 requests per window
});

app.use(limiter);
```

Monitoring and Logging

Monitoring and logging are crucial for detecting and responding to security incidents.

Logging Security Events

Implement logging to track authentication attempts, API access, and error events. This helps identify suspicious activities and aids in forensic investigations.

- **Implementation**: Use structured logging frameworks like Winston or Morgan to log relevant security events.

Monitoring for Anomalies

Set up monitoring systems to alert you of unusual patterns, such as spikes in requests or failed login attempts. Consider using APM tools or services that can help detect anomalies.

Best Practices for API Security

- **Secure Sensitive Endpoints**: Ensure that sensitive endpoints (e.g., login, user data) are adequately protected with authentication and authorization.
- **Keep Dependencies Updated**: Regularly update libraries and frameworks to patch known vulnerabilities.
- **Conduct Regular Security Audits**: Perform security audits and vulnerability assessments on your API and underlying infrastructure.
- **Educate Developers**: Provide training for developers on secure coding practices and awareness of common vulnerabilities.
- **Implement CORS Policies**: Set Cross-Origin Resource Sharing (CORS) policies to control which domains can access your API.

Securing your RESTful API is critical for protecting sensitive data and maintaining trust with users. By implementing robust authentication and authorization mechanisms, ensuring data encryption, validating and sanitizing input, and monitoring your application, you can significantly enhance the security of your API.

Data Encryption Strategies

Data encryption is a crucial aspect of securing a RESTful API, as it protects sensitive information from unauthorized access and ensures data integrity during transmission and storage. This chapter will delve into various encryption strategies, focusing on best practices for implementing encryption in your API.

Understanding Data Encryption

Data encryption transforms readable data (plaintext) into an unreadable format (ciphertext) using algorithms and keys. Only authorized parties with the correct decryption key can convert ciphertext back into plaintext.

Types of Encryption

- **Symmetric Encryption**: Uses the same key for both encryption and decryption. It is fast and efficient for large amounts of data but requires secure key distribution.
- **Asymmetric Encryption**: Uses a pair of keys—a public key for encryption and a private key for decryption. This method is slower and is often used for secure key exchange and digital signatures.

Encryption in Transit
Using HTTPS

Transport Layer Security (TLS), previously known as SSL, encrypts data transmitted between clients and servers. Implementing HTTPS is a fundamental practice for protecting sensitive information.

- **Implementation**:

Obtain an SSL/TLS certificate from a trusted Certificate Authority (CA).

Configure your web server (e.g., Nginx, Apache) to use HTTPS, ensuring that all API requests are served securely.

```
server {
    listen 443 ssl;
    server_name yourdomain.com;

    ssl_certificate /path/to/certificate.crt;
    ssl_certificate_key /path/to/private.key;

    location / {
        proxy_pass http://localhost:3000;  # Your API server
```

```
    }
}
```

Secure API Communication

When integrating with external services, always use HTTPS to encrypt data in transit. Ensure that your API clients also validate SSL certificates to prevent man-in-the-middle attacks.

Encryption at Rest

Data at rest refers to stored data that is not actively being accessed or transferred. Encrypting data at rest protects sensitive information in databases and file systems.

Database Encryption

Most modern databases, including PostgreSQL and DynamoDB, offer built-in encryption features for data at rest.

- **PostgreSQL**: Use the pgcrypto extension for encrypting specific columns or tables.

```
CREATE TABLE users (
    UserID SERIAL PRIMARY KEY,
    UserName VARCHAR(50),
    Email VARCHAR(100),
    EncryptedPassword BYTEA
);
```

To encrypt data:

```
INSERT INTO users (UserName, Email, EncryptedPassword)
VALUES ('Alice', 'alice@example.com',
pgp_sym_encrypt('password123', 'your-secret-key'));
```

- **DynamoDB**: Enable encryption at rest when creating a table or up-dating its settings. DynamoDB uses AWS-managed keys by default but can also use customer-managed keys through AWS Key Management Service (KMS).

File System Encryption

For file-based data storage, use file system-level encryption to secure sensitive files. Options include:

- **Encrypting File System (EFS)**: Native to Windows systems for encrypting files and folders.
- **Linux Unified Key Setup (LUKS)**: A standard for Linux disk encryption.

Key Management

Effective key management is essential for maintaining encryption security. Poor key management can lead to unauthorized data access, even if the data itself is encrypted.

Key Rotation

Regularly rotate encryption keys to minimize the risk of compromise. Implement automated key rotation processes to reduce manual intervention.

Key Storage

- **Hardware Security Modules (HSMs)**: Use HSMs for secure key generation, storage, and management.
- **AWS KMS**: If using AWS services, AWS Key Management Service (KMS) provides a fully managed solution for key management.

Access Control for Keys

Limit access to encryption keys to authorized personnel only. Use role-based access control (RBAC) to enforce strict access policies.

Implementing Encryption in Your API

To effectively implement encryption in your RESTful API, follow these steps:

Define Sensitive Data

Identify which data needs encryption. This often includes:

- User credentials (e.g., passwords, API keys).
- Personal identifiable information (PII).
- Financial data.

Choose Encryption Algorithms

Select strong encryption algorithms that meet industry standards, such as:

- **AES (Advanced Encryption Standard):** A symmetric encryption standard that is widely used and highly regarded for its security.
- **RSA:** An asymmetric encryption algorithm often used for secure key exchange.

Implement Encryption and Decryption Logic

Incorporate encryption and decryption into your application logic. For example, use libraries like crypto in Node.js for symmetric encryption.

```
const crypto = require('crypto');

function encrypt(text, key) {
    const iv = crypto.randomBytes(16);
    const cipher = crypto.createCipheriv('aes-256-cbc',
    Buffer.from(key), iv);
    let encrypted = cipher.update(text, 'utf-8', 'hex');
    encrypted += cipher.final('hex');
    return iv.toString('hex') + ':' + encrypted;
}

function decrypt(text, key) {
    const parts = text.split(':');
```

```
    const iv = Buffer.from(parts.shift(), 'hex');
    const encryptedText = Buffer.from(parts.join(':'), 'hex');
    const decipher = crypto.createDecipheriv('aes-256-cbc',
    Buffer.from(key), iv);
    let decrypted = decipher.update(encryptedText, 'hex',
    'utf-8');
    decrypted += decipher.final('utf-8');
    return decrypted;
}
```

Monitor for Security Breaches

Implement monitoring to detect unauthorized access to sensitive data. Track access logs, and establish alerting mechanisms for unusual activity.

Compliance Considerations

When handling sensitive data, ensure that your encryption practices comply with relevant regulations and standards, such as:

- **GDPR**: General Data Protection Regulation for protecting personal data in the EU.
- **HIPAA**: Health Insurance Portability and Accountability Act for protecting healthcare information.
- **PCI DSS**: Payment Card Industry Data Security Standard for handling credit card information.

Data encryption is a vital component of securing your RESTful API. By implementing encryption strategies for data in transit and at rest, managing encryption keys effectively, and adhering to compliance requirements, you can protect sensitive information from unauthorized access and maintain user trust.

Compliance and Data Governance

Compliance and data governance are critical aspects of managing a

RESTful API, especially in today's data-driven landscape where regulations regarding data privacy and security are increasingly stringent. This chapter will explore the importance of compliance, key regulations that may apply to your API, and best practices for implementing effective data governance.

Understanding Compliance

Compliance refers to adhering to laws, regulations, and standards governing how organizations manage and protect sensitive data. Failing to comply can result in severe penalties, legal consequences, and damage to your organization's reputation.

Importance of Compliance

- **Legal Protection**: Compliance helps protect organizations from legal liabilities and potential lawsuits.
- **Customer Trust**: Demonstrating compliance can enhance customer confidence in your organization's ability to protect their data.
- **Market Advantage**: Compliance can serve as a differentiator in competitive markets, attracting customers who prioritize data security and privacy.

Key Regulations and Standards

Depending on your industry and the types of data your API handles, several regulations may apply. Here are some of the most significant:

General Data Protection Regulation (GDPR)

The GDPR is a comprehensive data protection regulation in the European Union that governs how personal data is collected, processed, and stored.

- **Key Principles**:
- **Data Minimization**: Collect only the data necessary for your purpose.
- **Transparency**: Inform users about how their data will be used.
- **User Rights**: Provide users with rights to access, correct, and delete their data.

Health Insurance Portability and Accountability Act (HIPAA)

HIPAA establishes standards for protecting sensitive patient information in the healthcare industry. It mandates secure handling of protected health information (PHI).

- **Key Requirements**:
- **Data Encryption**: Encrypt PHI during transmission and storage.
- **Access Controls**: Implement role-based access controls to limit who can access PHI.

Payment Card Industry Data Security Standard (PCI DSS)

PCI DSS is a set of security standards designed to ensure that all companies that accept, process, store, or transmit credit card information maintain a secure environment.

- **Key Requirements**:
- **Secure Network**: Use firewalls and encryption to protect cardholder data.
- **Regular Testing**: Conduct vulnerability assessments and penetration testing.

California Consumer Privacy Act (CCPA)

CCPA enhances privacy rights and consumer protection for residents of California, giving them greater control over their personal data.

- **Key Provisions**:
- **Right to Know**: Consumers have the right to know what personal data is collected and how it's used.
- **Right to Opt-Out**: Consumers can opt out of the sale of their personal information.

Implementing Data Governance

Data governance refers to the management of data availability, usability, integrity, and security within an organization. A strong data governance framework helps ensure compliance with regulations and enhances data quality.

Establishing Data Governance Policies

- **Define Roles and Responsibilities**: Assign data stewardship roles to ensure accountability for data management and compliance efforts.
- **Create Data Policies**: Develop policies that outline how data is collected, processed, stored, and shared. Ensure these policies align with regulatory requirements.

Data Classification

Implement a data classification scheme to categorize data based on its sensitivity and the level of protection it requires. Common classifications include:

- **Public**: Information that can be shared openly.
- **Internal**: Sensitive information that is not intended for public disclosure but does not require stringent protection.
- **Confidential**: Highly sensitive data that requires strict access controls and protection measures.

Implementing Data Security Measures

- **Access Control**: Use role-based access control (RBAC) to restrict access to sensitive data. Regularly review and update access permissions.
- **Data Encryption**: Encrypt sensitive data both in transit and at rest to protect it from unauthorized access.
- **Regular Audits**: Conduct regular audits of data access and usage to ensure compliance with policies and regulations.

Monitoring Compliance
Continuous Monitoring

Implement continuous monitoring practices to assess compliance with regulations and internal policies. Use automated tools to track data access, changes, and potential violations.

Reporting and Documentation

Maintain comprehensive documentation of compliance efforts, including policies, procedures, and audit logs. This documentation can serve as evidence during compliance assessments and audits.

Training and Awareness

Conduct regular training sessions for employees to raise awareness about compliance requirements and data governance practices. Ensure that team members understand their roles in protecting sensitive data.

Responding to Data Breaches

In the event of a data breach, it is crucial to have a response plan in place to minimize damage and ensure compliance with reporting requirements.

Incident Response Plan

Develop an incident response plan that outlines the steps to take in the event of a data breach. This plan should include:

- **Identification**: How to identify a potential breach.
- **Containment**: Steps to contain the breach and prevent further access.
- **Notification**: Procedures for notifying affected users and regulatory bodies as required by law.

Post-Incident Review

Conduct a thorough review after a data breach to identify the root cause, assess the impact, and improve security measures to prevent future incidents.

Compliance and data governance are essential components of securing your RESTful API and protecting sensitive data. By understanding relevant regulations, implementing effective data governance policies, and monitoring compliance efforts, you can minimize risks and maintain the trust of your users.

Handling Sensitive Data in DynamoDB and PostgreSQL

Managing sensitive data in databases such as DynamoDB and PostgreSQL is crucial for maintaining security, compliance, and user trust. This chapter will discuss best practices for handling sensitive data in both databases, focusing on data encryption, access controls, compliance considerations, and secure data management techniques.

Understanding Sensitive Data

Sensitive data refers to any information that, if disclosed, could result in harm to individuals or organizations. Examples include:

- Personally Identifiable Information (PII): Names, addresses, Social Security numbers, and other identifying information.
- Financial Data: Credit card numbers, bank account information, and transaction histories.
- Health Information: Medical records and health-related data.
- Authentication Credentials: Passwords, API keys, and tokens.

Best Practices for Handling Sensitive Data in DynamoDB
Data Encryption

Encrypting sensitive data in DynamoDB is essential to protect it from unauthorized access.

- **Encryption at Rest**: Enable encryption at rest for your DynamoDB tables. By default, DynamoDB uses AWS-managed keys, but you can also use customer-managed keys through AWS Key Management Service (KMS).
- **Client-Side Encryption**: For additional security, consider encrypting sensitive data before storing it in DynamoDB. This approach ensures that even if an attacker gains access to your DynamoDB table, they cannot read the sensitive data.

```
const crypto = require('crypto');

function encrypt(text, key) {
    const iv = crypto.randomBytes(16);
    const cipher = crypto.createCipheriv('aes-256-cbc',
    Buffer.from(key), iv);
    let encrypted = cipher.update(text, 'utf-8', 'hex');
    encrypted += cipher.final('hex');
    return iv.toString('hex') + ':' + encrypted;
}

const sensitiveData = encrypt('sensitive information',
'your-secret-key');
```

Access Controls

Implement strict access controls to restrict who can read and write sensitive data in DynamoDB.

- **IAM Policies**: Use AWS Identity and Access Management (IAM) to create policies that restrict access to specific DynamoDB tables and actions. Ensure that only authorized users and applications can access sensitive data.
- **Fine-Grained Access Control**: For more granular control, consider using DynamoDB's fine-grained access control features, which allow you to specify access permissions based on attributes within your items.

Compliance Considerations

When handling sensitive data in DynamoDB, ensure compliance with relevant regulations (e.g., GDPR, HIPAA).

- **Data Minimization**: Collect only the sensitive data necessary for your application.
- **User Rights**: Implement mechanisms to fulfill user requests regarding their data, such as data access, correction, and deletion.

Best Practices for Handling Sensitive Data in PostgreSQL
Data Encryption

Similar to DynamoDB, encrypting sensitive data in PostgreSQL is vital for protecting it.

- **Encryption at Rest**: PostgreSQL offers various methods for encrypting data at rest. You can enable Transparent Data Encryption (TDE) or use third-party tools like pgcrypto for column-level encryption.

```
-- Example of using pgcrypto to encrypt a password
CREATE EXTENSION pgcrypto;

INSERT INTO users (UserName, EncryptedPassword)
VALUES ('Alice', crypt('password123', gen_salt('bf')));
```

- **Encryption in Transit**: Always use SSL/TLS to encrypt data in transit between clients and PostgreSQL servers.

Access Controls

Implement robust access controls in PostgreSQL to protect sensitive data.

- **Role-Based Access Control (RBAC)**: Use PostgreSQL roles and privileges to manage access to sensitive tables. Grant permissions based on user roles, ensuring that only authorized users can access sensitive data.

```
-- Create a role and grant SELECT privilege
CREATE ROLE data_analyst;
GRANT SELECT ON sensitive_table TO data_analyst;
```

- **Row-Level Security (RLS)**: PostgreSQL supports row-level security, allowing you to define policies that restrict access to specific rows based on user attributes.

Compliance Considerations

As with DynamoDB, ensure compliance with data protection regulations when handling sensitive data in PostgreSQL.

- **Audit Logging**: Implement audit logging to track access to sensitive data and changes to user permissions. This helps with compliance audits and security investigations.

```
CREATE EXTENSION pg_audit; -- For PostgreSQL audit logging
```

Secure Data Management Techniques
Data Minimization
Collect and store only the data necessary for your application. Implement data minimization principles to limit the exposure of sensitive information.
Input Validation and Sanitization
Implement strict input validation and sanitization to prevent injection attacks. Use parameterized queries or prepared statements to safeguard against SQL injection vulnerabilities.
Regular Backups and Data Recovery
Regularly back up sensitive data and implement a robust data recovery plan. Ensure that backup data is also encrypted and access-controlled.
Incident Response Planning
Develop an incident response plan to address data breaches or security incidents involving sensitive data. The plan should outline steps for containment, notification, and remediation.

Handling sensitive data in DynamoDB and PostgreSQL requires a proactive approach to security and compliance. By implementing robust encryption strategies, access controls, and secure data management techniques, you can protect sensitive information from unauthorized access and ensure compliance with regulatory requirements.

Integrating with Frameworks

Popular Frameworks for API Development
Frameworks provide the tools and structure necessary for building robust, scalable, and maintainable APIs. This chapter will explore three popular frameworks for API development: **Express.js**, **Flask**, and **Spring Boot**. We will examine their features, strengths, and best practices for integrating them into your API development process.

Express.js
Overview
Express.js is a minimalist web framework for Node.js, designed for building web applications and APIs. It simplifies the process of handling HTTP requests and responses, making it a popular choice for developers looking to create RESTful APIs.

Key Features

- **Middleware Support**: Express.js uses middleware functions to handle requests. Middleware can be added at different stages of request processing, allowing for functionality such as logging, authentication, and error handling.
- **Routing**: The framework provides a robust routing system, enabling you to define routes for your API endpoints easily.
- **Template Engines**: Express.js supports various template engines, allowing for server-side rendering of HTML if needed.
- **Extensibility**: With a large ecosystem of third-party middleware and

libraries, Express.js can be easily extended to fit your application's needs.

Setting Up an Express.js API

Installation: To set up an Express.js project, create a new directory and initialize it with npm:

```
mkdir my-express-api
cd my-express-api
npm init -y
npm install express
```

Creating a Simple API: Create an index.js file and set up a basic API:

```
const express = require('express');
const app = express();
const PORT = process.env.PORT || 3000;

app.use(express.json()); // Middleware to parse JSON requests

app.get('/api/users', (req, res) => {
    res.json([{ id: 1, name: 'Alice' }, { id: 2, name: 'Bob' }]);
});

app.listen(PORT, () => {
    console.log(`Server is running on http://localhost:${PORT}`);
});
```

Middleware Example: Implement a simple logging middleware:

```
app.use((req, res, next) => {
    console.log(`${req.method} ${req.url}`);
    next(); // Pass control to the next middleware
});
```

Best Practices

- **Organize Your Code**: Structure your project using a modular approach, separating routes, controllers, and middleware for maintainability.
- **Error Handling**: Implement centralized error handling to catch and manage errors gracefully.
- **Security**: Use middleware such as helmet to secure HTTP headers and express-rate-limit to prevent abuse.

Flask

Overview

Flask is a lightweight web framework for Python that is well-suited for developing web applications and RESTful APIs. Its simplicity and flexibility make it a popular choice among developers who prefer a minimalist framework.

Key Features

- **Lightweight and Simple**: Flask has a small core, making it easy to learn and use while allowing developers to add extensions as needed.
- **RESTful Request Dispatching**: Flask supports RESTful routing and request handling, making it ideal for building APIs.
- **Built-in Development Server**: Flask includes a built-in development server, enabling rapid development and testing.
- **Extensibility**: A rich ecosystem of extensions is available for adding functionality such as authentication, database integration, and validation.

Setting Up a Flask API

Installation: Install Flask using pip:

```
pip install Flask
```

Creating a Simple API: Create a app.py file and set up a basic API:

```
from flask import Flask, jsonify

app = Flask(__name__)

@app.route('/api/users', methods=['GET'])
def get_users():
    return jsonify([{ 'id': 1, 'name': 'Alice' }, { 'id': 2,
    'name': 'Bob' }])

if __name__ == '__main__':
    app.run(port=5000)
```

Using Flask Extensions: Install and use Flask extensions for additional features:

```
pip install Flask-SQLAlchemy
```

Example of using SQLAlchemy for database integration:

```
from flask_sqlalchemy import SQLAlchemy

app.config['SQLALCHEMY_DATABASE_URI'] = 'sqlite:///site.db'
db = SQLAlchemy(app)
```

Best Practices

- **Blueprints**: Use Flask Blueprints to organize your application into modules for better maintainability.
- **Error Handling**: Implement custom error handlers for different HTTP error codes to improve user experience.
- **Configuration Management**: Use environment variables and separate configuration files for different environments (development, testing, production).

Spring Boot
Overview
Spring Boot is a powerful framework for building enterprise-level applications in Java. It simplifies the development process by providing a suite of tools for creating stand-alone, production-grade Spring applications.

Key Features

- **Convention over Configuration**: Spring Boot follows the principle of convention over configuration, allowing developers to focus on writing code rather than configuring XML files.
- **Embedded Server**: Spring Boot includes an embedded server (like Tomcat or Jetty), making it easy to run and deploy applications.
- **Dependency Management**: It offers a built-in dependency management system, simplifying the process of adding and managing libraries.
- **Robust Ecosystem**: Being part of the larger Spring ecosystem, Spring Boot integrates seamlessly with various Spring projects, such as Spring Data, Spring Security, and Spring Cloud.

Setting Up a Spring Boot API
Create a Spring Boot Project: Use the Spring Initializr (https://start.spring.io/) to generate a new Spring Boot project with the necessary dependencies, such as Spring Web.

Project Structure: After generating the project, open it in your preferred IDE. The structure will look like this:

```
css
Copy code
src └──────
  main ├──────
     java │ └──────
       com │ └──────
          example │ └──────
             demo │ └──────
                DemoApplication.java └──────
        resources └──────
             application.properties
```

Creating a Simple API: Implement a basic RESTful API in DemoApplicati on.java:

```java
import org.springframework.boot.SpringApplication;
import
org.springframework.boot.autoconfigure.SpringBootApplication;
import org.springframework.web.bind.annotation.GetMapping;
import org.springframework.web.bind.annotation.RestController;

import java.util.List;

@SpringBootApplication
public class DemoApplication {
    public static void main(String[] args) {
        SpringApplication.run(DemoApplication.class, args);
    }
}

@RestController
class UserController {
    @GetMapping("/api/users")
    public List<User> getUsers() {
        return List.of(new User(1, "Alice"), new User(2, "Bob"));
    }
}
```

```
class User {
    private int id;
    private String name;

    public User(int id, String name) {
        this.id = id;
        this.name = name;
    }

    // Getters and setters
}
```

Best Practices

- **Profiles**: Use Spring Profiles to manage different configurations for various environments (e.g., development, testing, production).
- **Exception Handling**: Implement a global exception handler using @ControllerAdvice to manage exceptions and provide consistent error responses.
- **Security**: Integrate Spring Security for authentication and authorization, ensuring your API is secure from unauthorized access.

Choosing the right framework for API development depends on various factors, including language preference, project requirements, and team expertise. Express.js, Flask, and Spring Boot each offer unique features and benefits that cater to different development needs.

Best Practices for Integration

Integrating various components of a RESTful API, including frameworks, databases, and third-party services, is crucial for creating a seamless and efficient application. Adhering to best practices during the integration process can significantly enhance the maintainability, performance, and security of your API. This chapter outlines essential best practices for integration in API development.

Consistent API Design
Follow RESTful Principles

Ensure that your API adheres to RESTful principles, which include using standard HTTP methods (GET, POST, PUT, DELETE), proper use of status codes, and consistent resource naming conventions.

- **Resource Naming**: Use nouns for resource endpoints (e.g., /users, /orders) and plural forms for consistency.

Use Versioning

Implement API versioning to manage changes and maintain backward compatibility. This practice allows clients to continue using older versions of the API while you introduce new features.

- **Example of URI Versioning**:

```
/api/v1/users
/api/v2/users
```

Error Handling and Responses
Standardize Error Responses

Create a consistent error response format that provides meaningful information to clients. This can include an error code, message, and any relevant details.

- **Example of an Error Response**:

```json
{
    "error": {
        "code": "USER_NOT_FOUND",
        "message": "The user with the specified ID does not
        exist.",
        "status": 404
    }
}
```

Use HTTP Status Codes Appropriately

Return appropriate HTTP status codes for different outcomes, such as:

- 200 OK: Successful request.
- 201 Created: Resource successfully created.
- 400 Bad Request: Client error (e.g., invalid input).
- 401 Unauthorized: Authentication required.
- 403 Forbidden: Access denied.
- 404 Not Found: Resource not found.
- 500 Internal Server Error: Server error.

Security Considerations

Implement Authentication and Authorization

Secure your API using robust authentication and authorization mechanisms. Common methods include:

- **OAuth 2.0**: A widely used authorization framework that allows third-party services to exchange tokens securely.
- **JWT (JSON Web Tokens)**: A stateless authentication method that enables secure data transmission between parties.

Use HTTPS

Always use HTTPS to encrypt data in transit, protecting sensitive information from eavesdropping and man-in-the-middle attacks.

Rate Limiting and Throttling

Implement rate limiting to control the number of requests a client can make in a specified time period. This practice helps prevent abuse and mitigates denial-of-service attacks.

```
const rateLimit = require('express-rate-limit');

const limiter = rateLimit({
    windowMs: 15 * 60 * 1000, // 15 minutes
    max: 100 // Limit each IP to 100 requests per window
});

app.use(limiter);
```

Data Management and Validation
Input Validation

Validate incoming data to ensure it meets expected formats, types, and constraints. Use libraries such as Joi for Node.js or Marshmallow for Flask to enforce validation rules.

Sanitize Input

Sanitize user input to prevent injection attacks and ensure data integrity. Always escape special characters and strip out potentially harmful content.

Performance Optimization
Use Caching

Implement caching strategies to improve API performance and reduce load on databases. Use in-memory caching solutions like Redis or Memcached for frequently accessed data.

Optimize Database Queries

Analyze and optimize database queries to ensure they run efficiently. Use indexing, query optimization, and monitoring tools to identify slow queries and improve performance.

Documentation and Communication
Provide Comprehensive Documentation
Create detailed API documentation that includes:

- **Endpoint Descriptions**: Clear descriptions of available endpoints, including request/response formats and example payloads.
- **Authentication Methods**: Explain how to authenticate with the API.
- **Error Codes**: Document error codes and their meanings to help clients understand issues.

Tools like Swagger (OpenAPI) can help automate API documentation and provide an interactive interface for testing endpoints.
Communicate Changes Clearly
Inform clients about changes to the API, especially breaking changes or deprecations. Use changelogs and release notes to communicate updates effectively.

Testing and Quality Assurance
Automated Testing
Implement automated tests to ensure the reliability of your API. Focus on:

- **Unit Tests**: Test individual components and functions.
- **Integration Tests**: Test interactions between different components and external services.
- **End-to-End Tests**: Simulate real user scenarios to verify the overall functionality.

Tools like Jest, Mocha, or Postman can be used to automate testing processes.
Load Testing
Conduct load testing to evaluate how your API performs under heavy

traffic. Tools like Apache JMeter, Gatling, or Artillery can help simulate various load scenarios and identify potential bottlenecks.

Integrating various components of your RESTful API requires careful consideration of best practices to ensure a robust, secure, and maintainable application. By following these guidelines—ranging from consistent API design and error handling to security measures and performance optimizations—you can create a seamless integration experience for your API users.

Real-World Integration Examples

Integrating various technologies and frameworks is a critical part of building robust and efficient RESTful APIs. In this chapter, we will explore real-world integration examples that demonstrate how to leverage popular frameworks and services to create powerful APIs. We will look at how to integrate Express.js with MongoDB, Flask with SQLAlchemy, and Spring Boot with a third-party service.

Integrating Express.js with MongoDB
Overview

MongoDB is a popular NoSQL database that pairs well with Express.js, especially for applications requiring flexible schema designs and high scalability.

Example Setup

Install Dependencies: First, you need to install the necessary packages:

```
npm install express mongoose
```

Set Up the Express.js Application: Create a simple Express application that connects to MongoDB and defines a RESTful API for managing user data.

```
const express = require('express');
const mongoose = require('mongoose');

const app = express();
const PORT = process.env.PORT || 3000;

// Middleware
app.use(express.json());

// MongoDB connection
mongoose.connect('mongodb://localhost:27017/mydatabase', {
    useNewUrlParser: true,
    useUnifiedTopology: true
});

// Define a User model
const UserSchema = new mongoose.Schema({
    name: String,
    email: String
});

const User = mongoose.model('User', UserSchema);

// API endpoints
app.get('/api/users', async (req, res) => {
    const users = await User.find();
    res.json(users);
});

app.post('/api/users', async (req, res) => {
    const newUser = new User(req.body);
    await newUser.save();
    res.status(201).json(newUser);
});

app.listen(PORT, () => {
    console.log(`Server is running on http://localhost:${PORT}`);
```

```
});
```

Test the API: Use Postman or any API testing tool to test your API endpoints. You can create and retrieve users in your MongoDB database.

Integrating Flask with SQLAlchemy
Overview
Flask works exceptionally well with SQLAlchemy, a powerful ORM for managing relational databases in Python. This integration simplifies database operations while providing flexibility in data management.

Example Setup
Install Dependencies: First, install Flask and SQLAlchemy:

```
pip install Flask Flask-SQLAlchemy
```

Set Up the Flask Application: Create a Flask application that connects to a PostgreSQL database using SQLAlchemy.

```
from flask import Flask, jsonify, request
from flask_sqlalchemy import SQLAlchemy

app = Flask(__name__)
app.config['SQLALCHEMY_DATABASE_URI'] =
'postgresql://user:password@localhost/mydatabase'
db = SQLAlchemy(app)

# Define the User model
class User(db.Model):
    id = db.Column(db.Integer, primary_key=True)
    name = db.Column(db.String(50), nullable=False)
    email = db.Column(db.String(120), unique=True, nullable=False)

# API endpoints
```

```python
@app.route('/api/users', methods=['GET'])
def get_users():
    users = User.query.all()
    return jsonify([{'id': user.id, 'name': user.name, 'email':
    user.email} for user in users])


@app.route('/api/users', methods=['POST'])
def create_user():
    data = request.get_json()
    new_user = User(name=data['name'], email=data['email'])
    db.session.add(new_user)
    db.session.commit()
    return jsonify({'id': new_user.id, 'name': new_user.name,
    'email': new_user.email}), 201


if __name__ == '__main__':
    db.create_all()  # Create tables
    app.run(debug=True)
```

Test the API: Use Postman to test your Flask API by creating and retrieving users in your PostgreSQL database.

Integrating Spring Boot with a Third-Party Service
Overview
Spring Boot can be integrated with various third-party services to enhance functionality. In this example, we will integrate with a payment processing service (e.g., Stripe) to handle payments.

Example Setup
Create a Spring Boot Project: Use Spring Initializr to create a new project with dependencies for Spring Web and Spring Boot DevTools.

Add Stripe Dependency: Add the Stripe Java library to your pom.xml file:

```
<dependency>
```

```
        <groupId>com.stripe</groupId>
        <artifactId>stripe-java</artifactId>
        <version>latest.version</version>
    </dependency>
```

Set Up Application Properties: Configure your application properties (application.properties) to include your Stripe API key:

```
stripe.api.key=your_stripe_secret_key
```

Implement Payment Processing: Create a REST controller to handle payment requests:

```
import com.stripe.Stripe;
import com.stripe.model.Charge;
import com.stripe.param.ChargeCreateParams;
import org.springframework.beans.factory.annotation.Value;
import org.springframework.web.bind.annotation.*;

@RestController
@RequestMapping("/api/payments")
public class PaymentController {

    @Value("${stripe.api.key}")
    private String stripeApiKey;

    @PostMapping
    public String charge(@RequestBody ChargeRequest
    chargeRequest) {
        Stripe.apiKey = stripeApiKey;

        ChargeCreateParams params =
                ChargeCreateParams.builder()
                        .setAmount(chargeRequest.getAmount())
                        .setCurrency("usd")
```

```
                        .setSource(chargeRequest.getToken())
                        .setDescription("Payment for order")
                        .build();

        try {
            Charge charge = Charge.create(params);
            return charge.getId(); // Return the charge ID
        } catch (Exception e) {
            return e.getMessage(); // Handle exceptions
            appropriately
        }
    }
}

class ChargeRequest {
    private Long amount;
    private String token;

    // Getters and setters
}
```

Test the Payment API: Use Postman to test the payment processing endpoint by sending a POST request with the required payment details.

Integrating with various frameworks and services is essential for building powerful RESTful APIs. By leveraging Express.js with MongoDB, Flask with SQLAlchemy, and Spring Boot with third-party services, you can create robust applications that meet user needs.

Hybrid Architectures

Combining DynamoDB and PostgreSQL

As applications become more complex, leveraging the strengths of multiple databases can lead to enhanced performance, scalability, and flexibility. Hybrid architectures that combine NoSQL databases like DynamoDB with relational databases like PostgreSQL offer unique advantages, enabling developers to optimize their data management strategies according to specific use cases. This chapter explores the rationale behind using a hybrid approach, the benefits of combining DynamoDB and PostgreSQL, and best practices for integrating both databases into a cohesive architecture.

Understanding the Need for Hybrid Architectures
Diverse Data Requirements
Different data types and workloads often necessitate varied storage solutions. For instance:

- **Structured Data**: Relational databases like PostgreSQL excel in managing structured data with complex relationships, such as transactions and user data.
- **Unstructured or Semi-Structured Data**: NoSQL databases like DynamoDB are better suited for unstructured or semi-structured data, offering flexibility in data models that can evolve over time.

239

Performance and Scalability

A hybrid architecture allows applications to utilize the strengths of each database:

- **DynamoDB** provides automatic scaling and high availability, making it ideal for handling large volumes of traffic and unstructured data.
- **PostgreSQL** offers robust transactional support and ACID compliance, ensuring data integrity for critical operations.

Benefits of Combining DynamoDB and PostgreSQL
Flexibility in Data Modeling

Using both databases allows for flexible data modeling, enabling you to choose the most appropriate storage method for each type of data:

- Store user profiles and transactional data in PostgreSQL for structured access.
- Store session data, logs, or user activity data in DynamoDB for rapid access and scalability.

Optimized Performance

By distributing workloads across databases, you can optimize performance:

- Use DynamoDB for read-heavy workloads where high throughput and low latency are essential.
- Leverage PostgreSQL for complex queries and joins that require relational integrity.

Cost-Effectiveness

Using both databases can lead to cost savings by optimizing resource utilization:

- DynamoDB's pay-as-you-go pricing model can help reduce costs for variable workloads.

- PostgreSQL can be hosted on a more cost-effective infrastructure for transactional workloads, especially for applications with predictable usage patterns.

Architectural Patterns for Hybrid Integration

Integrating DynamoDB and PostgreSQL can be achieved through various architectural patterns, each suited to different application requirements:

Data Partitioning

Data partitioning involves distributing data across both databases based on specific criteria. For example:

- Store user-related data, such as profiles and preferences, in PostgreSQL.
- Store logs, activity streams, or analytics data in DynamoDB.

This approach ensures that each database is utilized according to its strengths while maintaining a clear separation of data.

Data Synchronization

Data synchronization techniques allow for consistent data across both databases, ensuring that updates in one database are reflected in the other:

- **Batch Synchronization**: Periodically synchronize data between PostgreSQL and DynamoDB. This can be achieved through scheduled jobs or ETL processes.
- **Real-Time Synchronization**: Implement event-driven architectures using AWS Lambda or other serverless technologies to trigger updates in one database based on changes in the other. For example, when a new user is created in PostgreSQL, a corresponding entry can be created in DynamoDB.

API Gateway Integration

Using an API gateway can facilitate communication between your application and both databases, providing a unified interface for data access:

- Create RESTful endpoints that abstract the complexity of managing two different databases.
- Use the API gateway to route requests to the appropriate database based on the data type or operation.

Best Practices for Integrating DynamoDB and PostgreSQL
Choose the Right Use Cases
Before implementing a hybrid architecture, evaluate the use cases that benefit from this approach. Common scenarios include:

- Applications that require both transactional integrity and scalability.
- Systems that need to handle diverse data types and workloads efficiently.

Maintain Data Consistency
Implement strategies to ensure data consistency across both databases:

- Utilize eventual consistency models when appropriate, particularly in scenarios where real-time updates are not critical.
- Use strong consistency models in PostgreSQL for critical transactions that require immediate data integrity.

Monitor Performance and Costs
Regularly monitor the performance and costs associated with both databases:

- Utilize tools like AWS CloudWatch for DynamoDB and pgAdmin or Datadog for PostgreSQL to track metrics and identify potential bottlenecks.
- Analyze cost patterns to ensure that your hybrid architecture remains cost-effective.

Implement Security Measures
Ensure robust security measures are in place for both databases:

- Use IAM roles and policies to manage access to DynamoDB.
- Implement role-based access control and encryption for PostgreSQL.

Document the Architecture

Maintain comprehensive documentation of your hybrid architecture, including:

- Data flow diagrams that illustrate how data is partitioned and synchronized between databases.
- API documentation that describes how clients interact with the system.

Real-World Example: E-Commerce Application

To illustrate the benefits of combining DynamoDB and PostgreSQL, consider an e-commerce application that manages product data, user profiles, and transactional information:

- **PostgreSQL**: Store user profiles, orders, and transactional data to ensure ACID compliance and facilitate complex queries (e.g., retrieving user order history).
- **DynamoDB**: Use for storing product catalog data, inventory levels, and user activity logs to benefit from rapid scaling and high throughput during peak shopping seasons.

Integration:

- Upon a new order in PostgreSQL, trigger a Lambda function that updates inventory levels in DynamoDB.
- Use an API gateway to route product queries to DynamoDB while user profile and order queries go to PostgreSQL.

Combining DynamoDB and PostgreSQL in a hybrid architecture enables developers to leverage the strengths of both databases, optimizing performance, scalability, and flexibility. By carefully selecting use cases, implementing robust data synchronization methods, and following best practices, organizations can create powerful applications that meet diverse data management needs.

Use Cases for Hybrid Approaches

Hybrid architectures that combine different types of databases, such as NoSQL databases like DynamoDB and relational databases like PostgreSQL, can significantly enhance application performance, flexibility, and scalability. This chapter will explore several use cases where hybrid approaches provide unique advantages, allowing developers to optimize data management strategies based on specific requirements.

E-Commerce Applications
Overview

E-commerce applications require handling diverse data types, including product catalogs, user accounts, orders, and transaction histories. The need for quick access to frequently updated data while maintaining data integrity makes a hybrid approach particularly beneficial.

Use Case Implementation

- **PostgreSQL**: Store user profiles, order history, and payment transactions. Its ACID compliance ensures the integrity of transactional operations.
- **DynamoDB**: Use for product catalogs and real-time inventory management. The ability to scale seamlessly during high-traffic events (e.g., Black Friday sales) allows the application to handle fluctuations in demand.
- **Integration Example**: When a user places an order, the application updates PostgreSQL to reflect the order details and triggers an update to DynamoDB to adjust the inventory levels in real time.

Content Management Systems (CMS)
Overview
Content management systems often manage various data types, including structured content (articles, posts) and unstructured data (media files, logs). A hybrid approach allows for efficient storage and retrieval of both data types.

Use Case Implementation

- **PostgreSQL**: Store structured content with relationships (e.g., user-generated content, comments, and categories) in a relational format.
- **DynamoDB**: Handle unstructured data like media files, user sessions, or logs that require high availability and rapid access.
- **Integration Example**: When new content is created, store metadata (e.g., title, author, publish date) in PostgreSQL and the associated media (e.g., images, videos) in DynamoDB. This separation allows for quick retrieval of media without affecting the performance of structured queries.

IoT Applications
Overview
Internet of Things (IoT) applications generate vast amounts of data from connected devices. These applications require robust solutions for handling time-series data, user interactions, and device management.

Use Case Implementation

- **DynamoDB**: Store time-series data from IoT devices, such as sensor readings, device states, and logs. The ability to handle high write throughput and low latency is essential for real-time data ingestion.
- **PostgreSQL**: Manage user profiles, device metadata, and configurations in a structured format. This ensures data integrity and enables complex queries on device interactions.
- **Integration Example**: Sensor data from devices is sent to DynamoDB for real-time processing, while device configuration settings are stored

in PostgreSQL. When a device sends a reading, an API call updates the device state in PostgreSQL and triggers analytics in DynamoDB.

Financial Services

Overview

Financial applications must manage sensitive information, adhere to regulatory compliance, and ensure data integrity. A hybrid architecture allows for optimal management of structured financial data while handling unstructured logs and transaction history.

Use Case Implementation

- **PostgreSQL**: Store structured financial data such as accounts, transactions, and user profiles. Its transactional capabilities and robust security features are critical for maintaining data integrity.
- **DynamoDB**: Use for handling logs, analytics data, and real-time monitoring of transactions. The scalability and quick access make it suitable for high-frequency trading scenarios.
- **Integration Example**: When a transaction occurs, the financial application logs the event in DynamoDB for real-time analytics while simultaneously updating the transaction details in PostgreSQL for compliance and auditing purposes.

Real-Time Analytics

Overview

Applications that require real-time analytics benefit from hybrid architectures that can handle both high-volume data ingestion and complex queries. Combining the strengths of DynamoDB and PostgreSQL allows for optimal data processing and reporting.

Use Case Implementation

- **DynamoDB**: Capture and store high-velocity event streams, user interactions, and operational metrics. Its ability to scale horizontally supports real-time data ingestion.

- **PostgreSQL**: Use for complex analytical queries and reporting. Its powerful querying capabilities are well-suited for aggregating and analyzing structured data.
- **Integration Example**: Event data is continuously ingested into DynamoDB, where it can be quickly accessed for real-time dashboards. Periodically, this data is aggregated and moved into PostgreSQL for in-depth analysis and reporting.

Gaming Applications
Overview
Gaming applications often involve managing user accounts, game states, scores, and player interactions in real time. A hybrid approach can effectively manage the diverse data requirements of modern gaming environments.

Use Case Implementation

- **PostgreSQL**: Store user accounts, profiles, achievements, and transactional data. The relational model allows for complex queries related to user interactions and game mechanics.
- **DynamoDB**: Handle real-time game state data, leaderboard rankings, and session data. The ability to scale and quickly update data is crucial for multiplayer experiences.
- **Integration Example**: When a player achieves a high score, the application updates the score in DynamoDB for immediate leaderboard visibility while also recording the achievement in PostgreSQL for historical tracking.

Hybrid architectures that combine DynamoDB and PostgreSQL offer a flexible, scalable, and efficient solution for a variety of applications. By leveraging the strengths of both databases, developers can create systems that meet diverse data management needs, optimize performance, and enhance user experiences.

Architectural Patterns for Hybrid Solutions

Creating a hybrid architecture that combines different types of databases, such as DynamoDB and PostgreSQL, requires careful consideration of architectural patterns. These patterns help ensure that the integration between the two systems is seamless, efficient, and maintainable. This chapter explores several architectural patterns suitable for hybrid solutions, discussing their implementation, advantages, and best practices.

Microservices Architecture

Overview

In a microservices architecture, applications are structured as a collection of loosely coupled services, each responsible for a specific business capability. This approach allows teams to develop, deploy, and scale services independently, making it an excellent fit for hybrid architectures.

Implementation

- **Service Design**: Each microservice can choose the most appropriate database for its needs. For instance, a user service might use PostgreSQL for relational data, while a product catalog service could utilize DynamoDB for fast lookups and scalability.
- **API Gateway**: Implement an API gateway to manage and route requests between clients and microservices. The gateway can handle authentication, logging, and request transformation.
- **Inter-Service Communication**: Use lightweight protocols such as REST or gRPC for communication between services. For data synchronization, consider using message queues (e.g., RabbitMQ, Kafka) to decouple services and improve scalability.

Advantages

- **Scalability**: Individual services can scale independently based on their database requirements and load.
- **Flexibility**: Teams can choose the best database for their specific use

case without impacting other services.

- **Resilience**: Failures in one service do not directly affect others, enhancing overall system reliability.

Event-Driven Architecture
Overview

Event-driven architecture (EDA) relies on events to trigger actions and communicate between different parts of an application. This pattern is especially useful for hybrid architectures, as it enables real-time data synchronization and decoupling between systems.

Implementation

- **Event Producers and Consumers**: Define event producers (e.g., services generating data) and consumers (e.g., services that react to events). For example, when a user is created in PostgreSQL, an event can be published to a message broker.
- **Message Broker**: Use a message broker (e.g., Apache Kafka, AWS SNS/SQS) to handle the transmission of events between services. This allows for reliable, asynchronous communication and reduces direct dependencies between services.
- **Data Synchronization**: Implement consumers that listen for specific events and update the corresponding database. For instance, a user registration event can trigger an update in both PostgreSQL and DynamoDB.

Advantages

- **Loose Coupling**: Services are decoupled from one another, allowing for easier maintenance and updates.
- **Real-Time Processing**: Data can be processed in real time, providing immediate updates across systems.
- **Scalability**: The architecture can easily scale to handle increased event loads by adding more consumers or partitions.

Data Federation
Overview
Data federation allows applications to access data from multiple sources as if it were coming from a single source. This approach is beneficial when integrating different databases in a hybrid architecture.

Implementation

- **API Layer**: Create an API layer that abstracts the complexity of accessing multiple databases. This layer can handle routing requests to the appropriate database based on the data type being requested.
- **Unified Data Model**: Define a unified data model that maps data from various sources, allowing for consistent access patterns across different systems.
- **Query Optimization**: Implement caching mechanisms and query optimization techniques to enhance performance when accessing data from multiple sources.

Advantages

- **Simplified Access**: Clients can access data from multiple databases without needing to understand the underlying architecture.
- **Increased Flexibility**: Data sources can be added or removed with minimal disruption to the overall system.
- **Reduced Complexity**: The application can focus on business logic rather than managing multiple data access layers.

Hybrid Storage Pattern
Overview
The hybrid storage pattern combines multiple data storage solutions to optimize data management based on data types and access patterns. This pattern allows for storing different data types in the most suitable database.

Implementation

- **Data Partitioning**: Partition data based on its nature. For example, store structured user data in PostgreSQL and unstructured log data in DynamoDB.
- **Data Duplication**: In some cases, it may be beneficial to duplicate certain data across databases to optimize read performance. For instance, user profiles may be stored in PostgreSQL, while relevant user activity logs can be stored in DynamoDB for fast access.
- **Data Flow Management**: Implement data flow management strategies to ensure that data is consistent across both databases. This may include periodic synchronization processes or real-time data updates through event-driven approaches.

Advantages

- **Optimized Performance**: Data is stored in the database that best suits its access patterns, improving performance.
- **Scalability**: Each database can scale independently based on its workload, providing efficient resource utilization.
- **Enhanced Flexibility**: The architecture can evolve with changing data requirements, allowing for easier integration of new data sources.

Hybrid architectures that combine DynamoDB and PostgreSQL offer unique advantages in terms of scalability, performance, and flexibility. By adopting appropriate architectural patterns—such as microservices, event-driven architecture, data federation, and hybrid storage—you can create robust systems that meet diverse data management needs.

Case Studies

Real-World Applications Using DynamoDB
DynamoDB, Amazon's fully managed NoSQL database service, is designed for high scalability, low-latency performance, and flexible data models. Its features make it particularly well-suited for various applications across industries. This chapter will explore several real-world case studies that highlight the successful implementation of DynamoDB in different scenarios.

Case Study: Amazon Prime Video
Overview
Amazon Prime Video, a popular streaming service, relies heavily on DynamoDB to manage its extensive catalog of movies and TV shows, user preferences, and viewing history. With millions of users streaming content simultaneously, the need for a highly scalable and reliable database is critical.
Implementation

- **Data Model**: Amazon Prime Video uses a denormalized data model in DynamoDB to optimize read performance. For instance, user preferences, viewing history, and recommendations are stored in a single table that leverages composite keys.
- **Caching**: To reduce latency and improve the user experience, Amazon Prime Video integrates DynamoDB with Amazon ElastiCache, providing fast access to frequently accessed data.
- **Event-Driven Architecture**: The service utilizes an event-driven

architecture where user interactions, such as adding items to watchlists, trigger updates to DynamoDB in real-time.

Outcomes

- **Scalability**: DynamoDB's ability to automatically scale to handle millions of concurrent users has been pivotal in maintaining performance during peak traffic events, such as new show releases.
- **Low Latency**: The combination of DynamoDB with caching layers ensures that user interactions are processed with minimal latency, resulting in a smooth streaming experience.

Case Study: Lyft
Overview
Lyft, a ride-sharing platform, utilizes DynamoDB to manage critical real-time data, including ride requests, driver availability, and customer feedback. The ability to handle high volumes of data while ensuring low latency is vital for their operational efficiency.

Implementation

- **Real-Time Data Processing**: Lyft employs DynamoDB to store real-time ride requests and status updates. The database's high write throughput capability allows it to process thousands of ride requests per second.
- **Geospatial Queries**: With the need for location-based services, Lyft integrates geospatial indexing to efficiently query driver availability based on geographic location.
- **Dynamic Pricing**: DynamoDB supports the storage of pricing models that change based on demand and supply conditions. This flexibility allows Lyft to quickly adjust fares during peak hours.

Outcomes

- **High Availability**: Using DynamoDB's multi-region replication, Lyft ensures that their data remains available even in the face of regional outages, enhancing overall service reliability.
- **Performance Improvement**: The low-latency nature of DynamoDB has improved the user experience significantly, allowing customers to receive ride updates in real-time.

Case Study: Samsung SmartThings
Overview
Samsung SmartThings is a smart home platform that connects various devices, such as lights, thermostats, and cameras, into a single ecosystem. DynamoDB plays a crucial role in managing device states, user settings, and event logs.

Implementation

- **Device State Management**: SmartThings uses DynamoDB to store the state of connected devices. Each device's status is quickly accessible, enabling seamless integration and control through the SmartThings app.
- **Event Logging**: The platform logs events generated by devices, such as motion detection or temperature changes, in DynamoDB. This allows users to review device activity and improve automation rules.
- **Scalability**: With the growing number of connected devices, Smart-Things leverages DynamoDB's scalability to manage the increasing volume of data without performance degradation.

Outcomes

- **Real-Time Control**: Users experience instant responses when interacting with their smart devices, thanks to the low-latency read and write capabilities of DynamoDB.
- **Efficient Data Management**: The platform efficiently manages vast amounts of event data, allowing users to monitor their smart homes

effectively.

Case Study: The Amazon Cloud Player
Overview

Amazon Cloud Player, a cloud-based music storage and streaming service, utilizes DynamoDB to manage user playlists, song metadata, and playback history. The ability to provide quick access to large datasets is crucial for a seamless music streaming experience.

Implementation

- **Playlist Management**: User playlists are stored in DynamoDB, allowing for quick retrieval and updates. The database structure supports a dynamic and flexible schema, which is essential for managing diverse music collections.
- **User Preferences**: DynamoDB tracks user listening habits and preferences to provide personalized recommendations and playback history.
- **Real-Time Synchronization**: Changes made to playlists or settings are updated in real-time across devices, ensuring a consistent user experience.

Outcomes

- **Personalized Experience**: By leveraging DynamoDB, Amazon Cloud Player can offer tailored recommendations based on user activity, enhancing engagement.
- **High Availability**: DynamoDB's automatic scaling and fault tolerance provide a reliable backend, ensuring that users can access their music collections anytime, anywhere.

These case studies demonstrate the versatility and power of DynamoDB in real-world applications. From streaming services like Amazon Prime Video to ride-sharing platforms like Lyft, and smart home integrations like Samsung SmartThings, DynamoDB provides the scalability, performance, and reliability required to handle diverse workloads.

Case Studies: Real-World Applications Using PostgreSQL

PostgreSQL is a powerful, open-source relational database known for its robustness, extensibility, and compliance with SQL standards. It is widely used in various industries for applications requiring complex queries, data integrity, and transactional support. This chapter explores several real-world case studies that highlight the successful implementation of PostgreSQL in diverse scenarios.

Case Study: Instagram
Overview
Instagram, the popular social media platform for sharing photos and videos, relies heavily on PostgreSQL to manage its massive amounts of user data, including profiles, posts, comments, and likes. The need for a robust and scalable database solution is critical given the platform's rapid growth and high user engagement.
Implementation

- **Data Model**: Instagram utilizes a relational schema in PostgreSQL to handle user accounts, posts, comments, and relationships between users. The structured nature of PostgreSQL allows for efficient management of these interconnected data types.
- **ACID Compliance**: The platform takes advantage of PostgreSQL's ACID (Atomicity, Consistency, Isolation, Durability) properties to ensure that transactions, such as liking a post or posting a comment, are processed reliably.
- **Geolocation Data**: Instagram also leverages PostgreSQL's PostGIS extension to manage geolocation data for geotagging posts, enabling users to discover content based on location.

Outcomes

- **Scalability**: PostgreSQL's ability to handle large volumes of data efficiently has supported Instagram's rapid user growth, allowing for seamless scaling.
- **Data Integrity**: The strict enforcement of data integrity constraints ensures that user data is consistent and reliable, fostering user trust in the platform.

Case Study: Spotify
Overview
Spotify, a leading music streaming service, utilizes PostgreSQL to manage its extensive catalog of songs, playlists, and user data. The need for complex querying capabilities and transactional support makes PostgreSQL an ideal choice for their backend.

Implementation

- **User Data Management**: Spotify stores user profiles, preferences, and playlists in PostgreSQL. The relational model allows for efficient querying and management of user relationships and interactions.
- **Analytics and Reporting**: Spotify uses PostgreSQL for analytics purposes, tracking user listening habits, song popularity, and engagement metrics. The database's robust querying capabilities enable detailed insights into user behavior.
- **Data Replication**: To ensure high availability and disaster recovery, Spotify implements database replication strategies, maintaining replicas of the PostgreSQL database in multiple regions.

Outcomes

- **Enhanced User Experience**: The ability to quickly retrieve user data and playlists leads to a seamless experience when users interact with the platform.

- **Robust Analytics**: The insights gained from analyzing user data allow Spotify to personalize recommendations, improving user engagement and satisfaction.

Case Study: Booking.com
Overview
Booking.com, a leading online travel agency, uses PostgreSQL to manage its extensive database of hotels, reservations, and user interactions. Given the high volume of transactions and complex queries, a reliable database system is crucial for their operations.

Implementation

- **Transactional Support**: Booking.com relies on PostgreSQL's transactional capabilities to handle reservations and cancellations securely, ensuring data integrity throughout the process.
- **Geospatial Queries**: The platform utilizes PostgreSQL's PostGIS extension to manage geospatial data for hotel locations, allowing users to search for accommodations based on their geographic preferences.
- **High Availability**: Booking.com employs a multi-node PostgreSQL setup with failover strategies to ensure high availability and reliability for their services.

Outcomes

- **Scalability**: PostgreSQL's performance allows Booking.com to handle millions of transactions daily without compromising on speed or reliability.
- **User Satisfaction**: The ability to provide real-time availability and accurate search results enhances user experience, leading to increased bookings.

Case Study: NASA
Overview

NASA utilizes PostgreSQL to manage vast amounts of data generated from various space missions and research projects. The need for a powerful and reliable database system is essential for storing and analyzing scientific data.

Implementation

- **Data Management**: NASA uses PostgreSQL to store mission data, research findings, and telemetry information. The relational capabilities allow researchers to perform complex queries and analyses on the data.
- **Data Integration**: PostgreSQL serves as a central repository for integrating data from various sources, including satellite data, research databases, and operational systems.
- **Open Source Contributions**: NASA actively contributes to the PostgreSQL community, enhancing features and performance while utilizing the database in their research.

Outcomes

- **Data Accessibility**: PostgreSQL's robust querying capabilities enable scientists and researchers to access and analyze data efficiently, fostering innovation and collaboration.
- **Reliable Data Management**: The reliability and performance of PostgreSQL ensure that mission-critical data is secure and consistently available for analysis.

Case Study: The United Nations

Overview

The United Nations (UN) employs PostgreSQL to manage various databases related to its global initiatives, including humanitarian aid, development programs, and peacekeeping efforts. The database plays a crucial role in data management and reporting.

Implementation

- **Data Aggregation**: The UN uses PostgreSQL to aggregate data from different projects and initiatives, allowing for comprehensive reporting and analysis.
- **Web Applications**: Various web applications developed by the UN use PostgreSQL as the backend database, providing access to vital information on projects, funding, and outcomes.
- **Compliance and Security**: PostgreSQL's strong security features, such as role-based access control, help the UN maintain compliance with data protection regulations.

Outcomes

- **Improved Decision-Making**: The ability to analyze aggregated data helps the UN make informed decisions regarding resource allocation and project management.
- **Transparency and Accountability**: PostgreSQL enables the UN to provide transparent reporting on its initiatives, fostering trust and accountability with stakeholders.

PostgreSQL's robust features and capabilities make it an ideal choice for various real-world applications, from social media platforms to scientific research and global organizations. The case studies presented in this chapter demonstrate how different organizations leverage PostgreSQL to manage complex data requirements, ensure data integrity, and enhance user experiences.

Lessons Learned from Successful Implementations

The case studies of organizations utilizing PostgreSQL and DynamoDB reveal valuable insights that can inform future database implementation strategies. Understanding the challenges faced and the solutions developed can help businesses make informed decisions when adopting or optimizing their database architectures. This chapter outlines key lessons learned from successful implementations of PostgreSQL and DynamoDB.

Scalability is Crucial
Anticipate Growth

Many organizations, such as Instagram and Lyft, experienced rapid growth, which placed a significant strain on their initial database setups. One of the most critical lessons learned is the importance of anticipating future growth when designing database architectures.

- **Lesson**: Choose a database solution that can easily scale horizontally (as seen with DynamoDB) or vertically (as PostgreSQL can be configured) to accommodate increasing data and user loads without significant rework.

Use Built-in Scalability Features

DynamoDB's automatic scaling capabilities have been pivotal for applications like Amazon Prime Video. Understanding and leveraging built-in features can alleviate the burden of manual scaling.

- **Lesson**: Utilize the built-in scalability features of your chosen database to streamline operations and ensure that performance remains optimal as demand fluctuates.

Performance Optimization is Ongoing
Monitor Performance Metrics

Applications like Spotify and Booking.com highlight the necessity of continuous performance monitoring. As usage patterns evolve, so too should optimization efforts.

- **Lesson**: Implement robust monitoring tools to track performance metrics and identify bottlenecks. Use this data to guide optimization efforts, whether through query tuning, index management, or cache strategies.

Optimize Data Models

The way data is structured significantly impacts performance. Both Spotify and NASA learned that an optimized data model is crucial for efficient querying.

- **Lesson**: Regularly review and refine your data model to align with usage patterns. Consider denormalization where necessary to improve read performance, especially for read-heavy workloads.

Data Integrity and Security are Paramount
Implement Robust Security Measures

Organizations like the United Nations have emphasized the importance of security when handling sensitive data. Using PostgreSQL's security features, such as role-based access control, is essential for protecting user information.

- **Lesson**: Always prioritize data security by implementing access controls, encryption, and regular security audits to protect sensitive data from unauthorized access.

Ensure Data Integrity

ACID compliance is a strong suit of PostgreSQL, as demonstrated by Booking.com. Ensuring data integrity during transactions is critical for maintaining user trust and operational reliability.

- **Lesson**: Choose a database that offers strong transactional support, particularly for applications requiring precise data integrity, such as financial services or user management systems.

Embrace Flexibility and Adaptability
Hybrid Solutions Can Offer Advantages

Many organizations have successfully leveraged hybrid architectures, as seen in case studies involving both DynamoDB and PostgreSQL. Combining the strengths of different databases can lead to optimized performance and resource utilization.

- **Lesson**: Consider a hybrid approach when dealing with diverse data requirements. Evaluate which database is best suited for specific use cases, and don't hesitate to use multiple systems to meet varied demands.

Foster a Culture of Continuous Improvement

Organizations such as NASA and the UN continually refine their systems to adapt to new challenges and technologies. The willingness to evolve is crucial for long-term success.

- **Lesson**: Cultivate a culture of continuous improvement within your development team. Encourage regular reviews of your database architecture and technologies to stay ahead of emerging trends and challenges.

Documentation and Communication
Maintain Clear Documentation

As highlighted in various case studies, maintaining comprehensive documentation is essential for both development and operational teams. Clear documentation aids in onboarding new team members and ensuring consistent practices.

- **Lesson**: Invest in high-quality documentation for your database architecture, API endpoints, and data models. Regularly update this documentation to reflect changes and improvements.

Communicate Changes Effectively

For organizations like Booking.com, communicating changes in data structures or API updates is vital for maintaining alignment across teams

263

and minimizing disruptions.

- **Lesson**: Establish clear communication channels and processes for sharing updates, ensuring that all stakeholders are informed and can adapt accordingly.

The successful implementations of PostgreSQL and DynamoDB across various industries offer valuable lessons that can guide future database architecture decisions. By prioritizing scalability, performance optimization, data integrity, security, flexibility, documentation, and communication, organizations can create resilient and effective database systems that meet evolving business needs.

Tools and Ecosystem

E ssential Tools for API Development
Building a robust API involves not just the choice of frameworks and databases but also a comprehensive ecosystem of tools that streamline development, testing, deployment, and monitoring. This chapter explores essential tools for API development, categorized into various stages of the development lifecycle, and highlights their features and benefits.

Development Tools

Integrated Development Environments (IDEs)

IDEs provide a comprehensive environment for writing, testing, and debugging code. Popular IDEs for API development include:

- **Visual Studio Code**: A lightweight, open-source code editor that supports numerous extensions for various programming languages, including JavaScript, Python, and Java. Features like IntelliSense, debugging tools, and Git integration make it a popular choice among developers.
- **PyCharm**: An IDE specifically for Python development, offering robust support for web frameworks like Flask and Django. Its powerful code analysis and debugging capabilities enhance productivity for Python developers.
- **IntelliJ IDEA**: A versatile IDE for Java and Kotlin development, particularly beneficial for working with Spring Boot. It provides powerful refactoring tools, code navigation, and integration with

version control systems.

Code Collaboration Tools

Collaboration tools facilitate team communication and version control during API development:

- **GitHub**: A widely used platform for version control using Git. It allows teams to collaborate on code, manage repositories, and track changes effectively.
- **GitLab**: Similar to GitHub, GitLab offers integrated CI/CD pipelines, issue tracking, and a comprehensive suite of DevOps tools, allowing teams to manage the entire development lifecycle.
- **Bitbucket**: A Git repository management solution that integrates with Jira, making it suitable for teams already using Atlassian products. Bitbucket provides features like pull requests and code reviews to enhance collaboration.

API Design and Documentation Tools
API Design Tools

Designing APIs involves creating specifications that define how the API will function. Tools for API design include:

- **Swagger (OpenAPI)**: An open-source framework for designing and documenting RESTful APIs. Swagger allows developers to define API endpoints, request/response formats, and authentication methods using a standardized format. The Swagger UI provides interactive documentation that facilitates testing and exploration.
- **Postman**: Initially a tool for testing APIs, Postman has evolved into a full-fledged API design tool that allows for defining, documenting, and testing APIs. It supports collaborative workspaces, enabling teams to design and refine APIs together.
- **Stoplight**: A platform that provides design-first API development, allowing teams to create API specifications using OpenAPI or GraphQL.

Stoplight offers visual tools for designing APIs and generating documentation automatically.

Documentation Tools

Clear documentation is essential for API usability. Tools that enhance API documentation include:

- **ReadMe**: A tool that enables developers to create beautiful, interactive API documentation. It provides features like versioning, code samples, and API reference guides that help developers understand and utilize the API effectively.
- **Redoc**: An open-source tool that generates documentation from OpenAPI specifications. Redoc offers a clean, user-friendly interface that can be easily integrated into existing applications.

Testing Tools
API Testing Tools

Testing APIs is critical to ensure they function correctly under various conditions. Key tools for API testing include:

- **Postman**: In addition to its design capabilities, Postman offers powerful testing features, including automated tests and integrations with CI/CD pipelines. Developers can write tests using JavaScript and run them as part of the testing workflow.
- **JMeter**: An open-source tool designed for performance testing and load testing of web applications, including APIs. JMeter allows users to simulate various types of requests and analyze performance metrics under load.
- **SoapUI**: A tool specifically designed for testing SOAP and REST APIs. It provides features for functional testing, security testing, and performance testing, making it suitable for comprehensive API testing.

Monitoring and Analytics Tools

API Monitoring Tools

Monitoring the performance and health of APIs is essential for maintaining service quality. Key monitoring tools include:

- **New Relic**: A powerful application performance monitoring (APM) tool that provides real-time insights into API performance, error rates, and transaction traces. New Relic helps identify bottlenecks and optimize performance.
- **Datadog**: An integrated monitoring platform that allows teams to track metrics, logs, and traces from APIs. Datadog provides customizable dashboards and alerts to help teams respond to issues proactively.
- **AWS CloudWatch**: A monitoring and observability service for AWS resources, including DynamoDB. CloudWatch provides metrics and logs to help monitor API performance and usage patterns.

Analytics Tools

Understanding how APIs are used can inform development and improvement efforts. Analytics tools include:

- **Google Analytics**: Although primarily used for web analytics, Google Analytics can be configured to track API usage by sending events from API calls. This helps teams understand user interactions and behaviors.
- **Mixpanel**: A product analytics tool that allows teams to track user actions and engagement with APIs. Mixpanel provides insights into how users interact with features, helping teams prioritize development efforts.

Deployment and DevOps Tools

Continuous Integration/Continuous Deployment (CI/CD)

Automating the deployment process enhances efficiency and reduces the risk of errors. Popular CI/CD tools include:

- **Jenkins**: An open-source automation server that supports building, testing, and deploying applications. Jenkins can be integrated with various plugins to streamline API deployment workflows.

- **GitLab CI**: A built-in CI/CD feature of GitLab that automates the testing and deployment of applications directly from the repository. It provides pipelines that can be customized for different deployment strategies.
- **CircleCI**: A cloud-based CI/CD service that automates the testing and deployment of applications. CircleCI integrates well with various code repositories and provides a user-friendly interface for configuring build pipelines.

Containerization and Orchestration

Containerization allows for consistent application environments, while orchestration manages those containers:

- **Docker**: A containerization platform that enables developers to package applications and their dependencies into containers. This ensures that APIs run consistently across different environments.
- **Kubernetes**: An orchestration platform that automates the deployment, scaling, and management of containerized applications. Kubernetes is ideal for managing microservices architectures and ensuring high availability.

The ecosystem of tools available for API development plays a crucial role in the success of any project. From development environments and design tools to testing frameworks and monitoring solutions, these tools streamline workflows, enhance collaboration, and improve overall efficiency.

Monitoring and Maintenance Tools

In the fast-paced world of API development, maintaining optimal performance and reliability is essential. Monitoring and maintenance tools help ensure that APIs function smoothly, provide insights into usage patterns, and enable prompt response to issues. This chapter will explore various tools available for monitoring and maintaining APIs, highlighting their features and benefits.

API Monitoring Tools
New Relic

- **Overview**: New Relic is a comprehensive application performance monitoring (APM) solution that provides real-time insights into the performance of applications, including APIs.
- **Key Features**:
- **Transaction Traces**: Detailed transaction traces allow developers to see how long each segment of an API request takes, helping identify bottlenecks.
- **Error Tracking**: Automatic error tracking provides insights into failures, allowing teams to respond quickly.
- **Dashboards**: Customizable dashboards display performance metrics such as response times, throughput, and error rates.
- **Use Case**: New Relic can be integrated into a web application to monitor API performance, enabling teams to optimize slow endpoints based on data-driven insights.

Datadog

- **Overview**: Datadog is a monitoring and analytics platform that provides visibility into application performance and infrastructure health.
- **Key Features**:
- **Integrated Metrics**: Collects metrics, traces, and logs in one place, providing a holistic view of API performance.
- **Alerts and Notifications**: Customizable alerts notify teams of performance issues or downtime.
- **APM Capabilities**: Datadog's APM features enable detailed monitoring

of request traces and dependencies.

- **Use Case**: Datadog can be employed by a microservices architecture to monitor multiple API endpoints, providing insights into cross-service performance and communication.

AWS CloudWatch

- **Overview**: AWS CloudWatch is a monitoring and observability service provided by Amazon Web Services that tracks resources and applications in real-time.
- **Key Features**:
- **Custom Metrics**: Users can define and monitor custom metrics for their APIs, such as latency, request counts, and error rates.
- **Logs and Insights**: Integrated log management allows for real-time analysis and troubleshooting of API performance issues.
- **Alarms**: Set alarms to trigger notifications based on specific thresholds, ensuring prompt responses to anomalies.
- **Use Case**: For applications hosted on AWS, CloudWatch can be used to monitor DynamoDB performance, Lambda functions, and other resources alongside API performance.

API Performance Testing Tools
Apache JMeter

- **Overview**: Apache JMeter is an open-source tool designed for performance testing and load testing of web applications, including APIs.
- **Key Features**:
- **Load Generation**: Simulates multiple users to test how well an API performs under stress.
- **Reporting**: Provides detailed reports on response times, throughput, and error rates, helping teams identify performance bottlenecks.
- **Extensibility**: Supports plugins for additional functionalities, including advanced reporting and custom scripting.

- **Use Case**: JMeter can be employed to conduct load tests on an API before deployment to ensure that it can handle expected traffic volumes.

Postman

- **Overview**: While primarily known for API testing and development, Postman also includes features for monitoring API performance.
- **Key Features**:
- **Automated Testing**: Allows users to create and run automated tests to verify API functionality and performance.
- **Monitor Collections**: Users can set up monitors to run collections at scheduled intervals, ensuring that APIs are functioning correctly over time.
- **Performance Reports**: Generates reports on response times, success rates, and failures for API requests.
- **Use Case**: Postman can be utilized to create a suite of automated tests that monitor the performance of APIs, providing insights into any degradation in response times or functionality.

Maintenance Tools
Log Management Tools
ELK Stack (Elasticsearch, Logstash, Kibana)

- **Overview**: The ELK Stack is a popular open-source solution for managing and analyzing log data.
- **Key Features**:
- **Centralized Logging**: Collects logs from various sources into a central location, making it easier to search and analyze log data.
- **Data Visualization**: Kibana provides a powerful interface for visualizing log data, enabling teams to identify trends and anomalies.
- **Real-Time Analysis**: Logstash processes log data in real-time, allowing for quick insights and troubleshooting.
- **Use Case**: The ELK Stack can be integrated into an API's infrastruc-

ture to aggregate and analyze logs from different services, aiding in debugging and performance monitoring.

Splunk

- **Overview**: Splunk is a powerful platform for searching, monitoring, and analyzing machine-generated data in real-time.
- **Key Features**:
- **Search Capabilities**: Offers advanced search and analysis capabilities to quickly sift through large volumes of log data.
- **Dashboards and Alerts**: Provides customizable dashboards and alerting features based on specific log patterns or errors.
- **Machine Learning**: Incorporates machine learning algorithms to predict issues and automate responses based on historical data.
- **Use Case**: Splunk can be used to monitor API logs, set alerts for error rates, and analyze user interactions with the API.

Database Monitoring Tools
pgAdmin

- **Overview**: pgAdmin is a popular open-source administration and management tool for PostgreSQL.
- **Key Features**:
- **Query Monitoring**: Provides tools for analyzing and optimizing SQL queries, helping maintain performance.
- **User Management**: Simplifies user management, roles, and permissions within PostgreSQL databases.
- **Dashboard**: Offers a dashboard to visualize database metrics and performance statistics.
- **Use Case**: pgAdmin can be used by database administrators to monitor and maintain PostgreSQL databases, ensuring optimal performance and data integrity.

DynamoDB Monitoring Tools
AWS CloudWatch for DynamoDB

- **Overview**: AWS CloudWatch can also be used specifically for monitoring DynamoDB tables.
- **Key Features**:
- **Table Metrics**: Tracks metrics such as read/write capacity, throttled requests, and latency for DynamoDB tables.
- **Alarms**: Set alarms for specific metrics to proactively manage performance issues.
- **Integration with Lambda**: CloudWatch can trigger AWS Lambda functions in response to specific events, allowing for automated responses to performance issues.
- **Use Case**: CloudWatch can be configured to monitor DynamoDB tables used in an application, allowing teams to respond to performance degradation or capacity issues in real-time.

Monitoring and maintenance tools are essential for ensuring the reliability, performance, and security of APIs. From monitoring tools like New Relic and Datadog to performance testing tools like Apache JMeter and Postman, each tool plays a critical role in the API development lifecycle.

Community Resources and Libraries

The strength of any technology ecosystem often lies in its community. For API development, numerous resources, libraries, and community contributions can significantly enhance productivity and foster innovation. This chapter highlights key community resources and libraries for both PostgreSQL and DynamoDB, showcasing how they can streamline development processes and provide additional functionality.

Community Resources
Documentation and Tutorials

- **PostgreSQL Documentation**: The official PostgreSQL documentation is comprehensive and includes everything from installation guides to advanced SQL topics. It is an invaluable resource for both beginners and experienced users.
- **DynamoDB Documentation**: Amazon provides extensive documentation for DynamoDB, including guides on data modeling, best practices, and API references. The documentation is essential for understanding the full capabilities of the service.
- **TutorialsPoint**: Offers tutorials for various technologies, including step-by-step guides on using PostgreSQL and DynamoDB, covering basic to advanced topics.
- **YouTube Channels**: Several YouTube channels, such as "Academind" and "Traversy Media," provide video tutorials on API development with PostgreSQL and DynamoDB, making it easier to grasp concepts visually.

Community Forums and Discussion Groups

- **Stack Overflow**: A vital resource for developers, Stack Overflow features a wealth of questions and answers related to PostgreSQL and DynamoDB. Engaging with the community can help resolve specific issues and foster learning.
- **PostgreSQL Mailing Lists**: PostgreSQL has dedicated mailing lists for different topics, where developers can discuss features, report bugs, and seek advice.
- **DynamoDB Developer Forum**: Amazon hosts a developer forum for DynamoDB where users can ask questions, share experiences, and connect with other developers working on similar projects.
- **Reddit Communities**: Subreddits like r/PostgreSQL and r/aws provide platforms for discussions, sharing resources, and asking questions about PostgreSQL and AWS services, including DynamoDB.

Libraries and Frameworks
PostgreSQL Libraries

- **SQLAlchemy**: A powerful SQL toolkit and Object-Relational Mapping (ORM) library for Python. SQLAlchemy allows developers to interact with PostgreSQL in a more Pythonic way, facilitating complex queries and relationships with ease.
- **pg-promise**: A PostgreSQL library for Node.js that provides a robust and flexible API for interacting with PostgreSQL. It supports promise-based queries, allowing for easier asynchronous programming.
- **Django ORM**: The built-in ORM for the Django web framework provides seamless integration with PostgreSQL. It allows developers to interact with the database using Python objects, simplifying data manipulation and queries.
- **node-postgres (pg)**: A PostgreSQL client for Node.js that provides a straightforward API for interacting with PostgreSQL databases. It supports both callback and promise-based queries, making it easy to integrate into various applications.

DynamoDB Libraries

- **AWS SDK for JavaScript**: The official SDK for JavaScript provides a simple way to interact with DynamoDB from Node.js applications. It includes methods for performing CRUD operations and querying data.
- **DynamoDB Document Client**: A part of the AWS SDK, the Document Client simplifies working with DynamoDB by abstracting away the complexities of data formatting and marshaling.
- **Dynamoose**: An ORM for DynamoDB designed for Node.js, Dynamoose allows developers to define schemas, perform validations, and interact with DynamoDB using a more intuitive interface.
- **Boto3**: The AWS SDK for Python, Boto3 allows developers to interact with various AWS services, including DynamoDB. It provides a comprehensive API for performing operations and managing resources.

Open Source Projects and Tools
Database Management Tools

- **pgAdmin**: An open-source administration and management tool for PostgreSQL, pgAdmin provides a graphical interface for managing databases, executing SQL queries, and monitoring performance.
- **DynamoDB Admin**: An open-source web-based tool for managing DynamoDB tables. It provides a user-friendly interface for viewing, creating, and modifying items in DynamoDB.

Data Migration Tools

- **AWS Database Migration Service (DMS)**: A fully managed service that helps migrate databases to AWS, including migrations to DynamoDB from various database engines, including PostgreSQL.
- **pgLoader**: An open-source data loading tool that can migrate data from various sources to PostgreSQL, allowing for efficient data transfer and transformation.

Learning and Certification Resources
Online Learning Platforms

- **Udemy**: Offers various courses on PostgreSQL and DynamoDB, covering topics from basic database management to advanced API development techniques.
- **Coursera**: Partners with universities to provide courses on database management and cloud services, including specific courses focused on PostgreSQL and AWS DynamoDB.
- **Pluralsight**: Provides a library of video courses on software development topics, including PostgreSQL and AWS, with a focus on practical implementation.

Certification Programs

- **AWS Certified Database – Specialty**: This certification demonstrates expertise in database services on AWS, including DynamoDB. It validates knowledge in database design, migration, and implementation.

- **PostgreSQL Certification**: Various organizations, including the PostgreSQL Global Development Group, offer certification programs for PostgreSQL, validating skills in database administration, development, and performance tuning.

The community resources and libraries available for PostgreSQL and DynamoDB significantly enhance the capabilities of developers and organizations. By leveraging these tools, developers can streamline their workflows, improve productivity, and foster collaboration.

Future Trends in API Development

Emerging Technologies
The landscape of API development is continually evolving, driven by advancements in technology and changing business needs. As organizations increasingly rely on APIs to connect services, manage data, and enhance user experiences, several emerging technologies are shaping the future of API development. This chapter explores key emerging technologies that are influencing API development, their implications, and how they can be leveraged to create more robust, efficient, and scalable APIs.

GraphQL

Overview

GraphQL is a query language for APIs developed by Facebook that allows clients to request exactly the data they need, minimizing over-fetching and under-fetching. Unlike traditional REST APIs, which expose fixed endpoints for specific resources, GraphQL provides a single endpoint that can serve various data requests.

Advantages

- **Flexible Queries**: Clients can specify the structure of the response, reducing the amount of data transferred and improving performance.
- **Strongly Typed Schema**: GraphQL uses a schema to define types and relationships, enabling better validation and documentation.
- **Introspection**: GraphQL APIs support introspection, allowing devel-

opers to explore available data types and queries programmatically.

Use Cases

GraphQL is particularly useful for applications with complex data needs, such as:

- **Mobile Applications**: Where minimizing bandwidth and improving response times are critical.
- **Single Page Applications (SPAs)**: That require dynamic data fetching based on user interactions.

API-First Design

Overview

The API-first design approach emphasizes the development of APIs before building applications or services that consume them. This methodology fosters collaboration between frontend and backend teams and aligns development efforts with business goals.

Advantages

- **Consistent Development**: Teams can work in parallel, ensuring that the API is designed to meet both current and future needs.
- **Improved Documentation**: Creating documentation alongside API design helps maintain clarity and reduces misunderstandings.
- **Enhanced Testing**: Early focus on API design enables teams to establish testing frameworks and protocols from the outset.

Use Cases

API-first design is beneficial in scenarios where:

- **Microservices Architecture**: Multiple services need to communicate efficiently and consistently.
- **Rapid Development Cycles**: Organizations need to pivot quickly based on changing business requirements.

Serverless Computing
Overview
Serverless computing allows developers to build and run applications without managing servers. Instead, the cloud provider dynamically allocates resources, enabling automatic scaling and reduced operational overhead. AWS Lambda, Azure Functions, and Google Cloud Functions are examples of serverless platforms that facilitate API development.

Advantages

- **Cost-Effective**: Organizations pay only for the compute time they consume, making it a cost-efficient solution for variable workloads.
- **Automatic Scaling**: Serverless architectures can automatically scale based on demand, ensuring high availability and performance.
- **Simplified Deployment**: Developers can focus on writing code and deploying functions without worrying about the underlying infrastructure.

Use Cases
Serverless computing is particularly suitable for:

- **Event-Driven APIs**: Where actions are triggered by specific events (e.g., file uploads, database changes).
- **Microservices**: Small, independently deployable services that can benefit from quick scaling and cost management.

API Management Platforms
Overview
API management platforms provide tools and services to design, publish, secure, and analyze APIs. These platforms help organizations manage the entire API lifecycle, from development to consumption.

Key Features

- **Security**: API management tools offer authentication, authorization, and traffic management features to protect APIs from abuse.

- **Analytics**: These platforms provide insights into API usage, performance metrics, and user engagement, allowing organizations to make data-driven decisions.
- **Rate Limiting and Throttling**: Management tools can enforce policies to control the rate of requests, ensuring fair usage and preventing server overload.

Popular Platforms

- **Apigee**: Google Cloud's API management platform, offering powerful analytics and security features.
- **AWS API Gateway**: A fully managed service that makes it easy to create, publish, maintain, monitor, and secure APIs at scale.
- **MuleSoft**: Provides comprehensive API management solutions along with integration capabilities across various systems.

API Security Enhancements
Overview

As the importance of APIs grows, so do the security challenges. Emerging technologies are focusing on enhancing API security to protect against various threats.

Key Technologies

- **OAuth 2.0 and OpenID Connect**: These protocols provide secure authorization and authentication for APIs, enabling users to grant third-party access without sharing credentials.
- **API Gateways**: Acting as a protective layer, API gateways enforce security policies, manage traffic, and authenticate requests before they reach backend services.
- **WAF (Web Application Firewalls)**: WAFs protect APIs from common attacks, such as SQL injection and Cross-Site Scripting (XSS), by filtering and monitoring HTTP traffic.

Importance of Security

API security is critical for protecting sensitive data and maintaining user trust. Organizations must adopt a proactive approach to securing APIs, including regular security audits and vulnerability assessments.

Low-Code and No-Code Platforms

Overview

Low-code and no-code platforms enable users to build applications and APIs with minimal or no coding experience. These platforms provide visual development environments and pre-built components that simplify the API development process.

Advantages

- **Accelerated Development**: Users can quickly prototype and deploy APIs without deep technical knowledge.
- **Increased Collaboration**: Business users can participate in the development process, bridging the gap between technical and non-technical stakeholders.

Popular Platforms

- **OutSystems**: A low-code platform for building applications that include API development capabilities.
- **Mendix**: Offers a visual development environment for creating applications and APIs quickly.

Artificial Intelligence and Machine Learning Integration

Overview

Integrating AI and machine learning capabilities into APIs is an emerging trend that enables organizations to leverage data-driven insights and automation.

Applications

- **Predictive Analytics**: APIs can be designed to provide predictive insights based on historical data, allowing businesses to make informed decisions.
- **Natural Language Processing (NLP)**: AI-driven APIs can facilitate interaction with users through natural language, enhancing user experience and engagement.

Examples

- **IBM Watson**: Offers APIs for various AI capabilities, including natural language understanding, speech recognition, and image analysis.
- **Google Cloud AI**: Provides a suite of machine learning APIs that developers can integrate into their applications to enhance functionality.

The future of API development is shaped by emerging technologies that enhance flexibility, scalability, and performance. From GraphQL and serverless computing to AI integration and low-code platforms, these advancements provide developers with the tools to build more efficient and robust APIs.

The Role of AI and Machine Learning in API Development

Artificial Intelligence (AI) and Machine Learning (ML) are revolutionizing various industries, and their integration into API development is no exception. APIs are essential for enabling communication between applications, services, and systems, and incorporating AI and ML capabilities into these APIs enhances their functionality, performance, and adaptability. This chapter explores the role of AI and machine learning in API development, including their benefits, applications, and future potential.

Enhancing API Functionality
Intelligent Data Processing

AI and ML can be leveraged to improve how APIs process and analyze data:

- **Natural Language Processing (NLP)**: APIs can utilize NLP to understand and interpret human language. This enables applications to provide functionalities like sentiment analysis, chatbots, and voice recognition.
- **Example**: A customer support API could analyze user queries to provide instant responses or escalate issues to human agents based on sentiment analysis.
- **Image and Video Analysis**: APIs can employ computer vision techniques to analyze and interpret visual data. This allows for tasks such as object detection, facial recognition, and image classification.
- **Example**: An e-commerce platform could use an image recognition API to identify products in user-uploaded photos, enhancing the shopping experience.

Personalization and Recommendations

AI and ML can enable APIs to provide personalized experiences:

- **Recommendation Engines**: APIs can analyze user behavior and preferences to deliver tailored content and product recommendations. By utilizing collaborative filtering and content-based filtering techniques, APIs can enhance user engagement.
- **Example**: Streaming services like Netflix use recommendation APIs to suggest shows and movies based on user viewing history and preferences.
- **Dynamic Pricing**: AI-driven APIs can adjust prices based on demand, competitor pricing, and customer behavior, optimizing revenue generation.
- **Example**: Travel booking platforms can use dynamic pricing APIs to offer competitive rates based on real-time market analysis.

Improving API Performance
Predictive Analytics

Integrating AI and ML into APIs allows for predictive analytics, which can enhance performance and decision-making:

- **Usage Prediction**: APIs can analyze historical usage patterns to forecast future demand. This helps in optimizing resource allocation and scaling, ensuring that the API performs efficiently during peak times.
- **Example**: A cloud service provider can use predictive analytics to dynamically allocate resources for APIs based on anticipated traffic spikes.
- **Anomaly Detection**: AI algorithms can monitor API traffic and identify unusual patterns that may indicate performance issues or potential security threats.
- **Example**: Anomaly detection APIs can alert developers to unusual spikes in error rates, allowing for quick remediation of underlying issues.

Automated Testing and Quality Assurance

AI and ML can enhance the testing process of APIs, leading to more robust and reliable applications:

- **Test Automation**: Machine learning algorithms can automate the generation of test cases based on historical API usage data. This reduces manual effort and ensures comprehensive test coverage.
- **Example**: An API testing tool could analyze past interactions to generate tests that simulate various user scenarios and edge cases.
- **Continuous Quality Improvement**: AI can analyze testing outcomes and provide insights for improving API performance and reliability, enabling continuous integration and delivery practices.

Streamlining API Development
Code Generation and Optimization

AI tools can assist in generating code and optimizing API development processes:

- **Automated Code Generation**: AI-powered tools can help developers write code faster by generating boilerplate code based on specifications or existing code patterns.
- **Example**: An API development platform may offer a code generation feature that creates RESTful endpoint definitions based on user-defined data models.
- **Code Review and Optimization**: Machine learning models can analyze code for best practices, suggesting optimizations and identifying potential vulnerabilities.
- **Example**: AI-driven code review tools can highlight performance bottlenecks or security risks in API code before deployment.

AI-Powered API Management
Intelligent API Gateways

AI can enhance the capabilities of API gateways, providing advanced features for management and security:

- **Traffic Management**: AI algorithms can analyze traffic patterns to optimize load balancing and resource allocation, ensuring high availability and performance.
- **Security Enhancements**: AI can detect and mitigate security threats in real-time, such as DDoS attacks or malicious requests, by analyzing request patterns and behaviors.

Use Cases of AI and ML in API Development
Chatbots and Virtual Assistants

Integrating AI-powered natural language processing APIs allows businesses to create chatbots and virtual assistants that can interact with users in real time. These APIs can analyze user input, understand intent, and generate appropriate responses, enhancing customer engagement and

support.
Fraud Detection and Prevention
Financial institutions leverage AI and ML APIs to analyze transaction data in real-time, identifying patterns indicative of fraud. By continuously learning from new data, these systems can adapt to evolving fraud tactics, providing enhanced security.

Predictive Maintenance
In industries like manufacturing and logistics, APIs that utilize AI can analyze sensor data from equipment to predict failures before they occur. This proactive approach minimizes downtime and reduces maintenance costs.

Health Monitoring
Healthcare applications can use AI-powered APIs to analyze patient data, providing insights for personalized treatment plans or alerts for potential health issues based on predictive modeling.

Challenges and Considerations
Data Privacy and Security
Integrating AI and ML into APIs raises concerns about data privacy and security. Organizations must ensure compliance with regulations such as GDPR and HIPAA when handling sensitive data.

Model Bias
AI and ML models can exhibit bias based on the data they are trained on. It's crucial for developers to regularly evaluate models to mitigate bias and ensure fairness in decision-making processes.

Complexity and Resource Requirements
Implementing AI and ML can add complexity to API development. Organizations must assess their infrastructure and resources to support these technologies effectively.

AI and machine learning are transforming the API landscape, enabling developers to create more intelligent, efficient, and responsive applications. By enhancing functionality, improving performance, and streamlining development processes, these technologies provide significant advantages in the competitive software development market.

Preparing for the Future of RESTful APIs

As the technology landscape continues to evolve, RESTful APIs remain a cornerstone of modern web development. However, to remain competitive and effective, developers and organizations must adapt to emerging trends, technologies, and best practices. This chapter explores how to prepare for the future of RESTful APIs, focusing on adaptation strategies, best practices, and the evolving role of APIs in software ecosystems.

Embrace API-First Development

What is API-First Development?

API-first development involves designing and building APIs before implementing the services that consume them. This approach fosters collaboration between teams and ensures that APIs are aligned with business goals from the outset.

Benefits of API-First Development

- **Clear Documentation**: Early API design leads to better documentation, making it easier for frontend and backend teams to align on requirements and usage.
- **Consistent Development**: Teams can work in parallel, with frontend developers consuming APIs while backend developers implement them.
- **User-Centric Design**: Focusing on API design encourages developers to consider the end-user experience, leading to more usable and effective APIs.

Action Steps

- **Define Clear API Specifications**: Use tools like OpenAPI Specification (OAS) to define APIs before development begins.

- **Collaborate Across Teams**: Foster communication between frontend and backend teams to ensure alignment on requirements and expectations.

Invest in Automation and CI/CD

The Role of Automation in API Development

Automation enhances efficiency, reduces errors, and speeds up the development lifecycle. Continuous Integration and Continuous Deployment (CI/CD) practices ensure that changes are tested and deployed quickly and reliably.

Benefits of CI/CD for APIs

- **Faster Development Cycles**: Automated testing and deployment pipelines allow for rapid iteration and deployment of API changes.
- **Improved Quality Assurance**: Automated tests help catch errors early, ensuring that APIs meet quality standards before deployment.
- **Consistent Environments**: CI/CD pipelines can ensure that APIs are tested in environments that closely mirror production.

Action Steps

- **Implement CI/CD Tools**: Use tools like Jenkins, GitLab CI, or CircleCI to automate the testing and deployment of APIs.
- **Create Automated Test Suites**: Develop comprehensive test suites to validate API functionality, performance, and security.

Focus on Security Best Practices

The Importance of API Security

As APIs become more integral to applications, they also become prime targets for attacks. Ensuring API security is paramount for protecting sensitive data and maintaining user trust.

Security Best Practices

- **Authentication and Authorization**: Implement robust authentication mechanisms (e.g., OAuth 2.0) and enforce strict authorization rules to control access to APIs.
- **Input Validation**: Validate all incoming data to prevent common attacks such as SQL injection and Cross-Site Scripting (XSS).
- **Rate Limiting**: Apply rate limiting to APIs to protect against abuse and DDoS attacks.

Action Steps

- **Conduct Regular Security Audits**: Regularly assess API security measures to identify vulnerabilities and improve defenses.
- **Stay Informed on Security Threats**: Keep up-to-date with the latest security trends and threats relevant to API development.

Leverage Emerging Technologies
Importance of Adapting to New Technologies

Emerging technologies such as AI, machine learning, and GraphQL are shaping the future of API development. Organizations should explore how these technologies can enhance their API offerings.

Opportunities for Integration

- **AI and ML Integration**: Consider incorporating AI-driven insights into APIs for predictive analytics, personalization, and enhanced user experiences.
- **Adopt GraphQL**: Explore GraphQL as an alternative to REST for applications that require flexible and efficient data retrieval.

Action Steps

- **Experiment with New Technologies**: Create proof-of-concept projects to evaluate the benefits of integrating new technologies into existing APIs.

- **Train Teams on Emerging Trends**: Invest in training and resources for development teams to stay informed about emerging technologies.

Enhance Monitoring and Analytics
The Role of Monitoring in API Management

Effective monitoring and analytics are essential for maintaining API performance and reliability. As usage patterns change, organizations must adapt their monitoring strategies accordingly.

Key Monitoring Metrics

- **Response Time**: Track average response times to ensure APIs meet performance benchmarks.
- **Error Rates**: Monitor error rates to identify and address issues promptly.
- **Usage Patterns**: Analyze API usage data to understand how clients interact with APIs and identify areas for improvement.

Action Steps

- **Implement Monitoring Tools**: Use tools like New Relic, Datadog, or AWS CloudWatch to gain insights into API performance and usage.
- **Establish KPIs**: Define key performance indicators (KPIs) to assess API success and inform optimization strategies.

Foster a Developer-Centric Culture
The Importance of Developer Experience

As the demand for APIs grows, providing a positive developer experience is crucial for adoption and satisfaction. Organizations should prioritize the needs of developers when designing and implementing APIs.

Strategies for Improving Developer Experience

- **Comprehensive Documentation**: Ensure that API documentation is clear, comprehensive, and easy to navigate.

- **Interactive API Testing Tools**: Provide tools like Postman or Swagger UI that allow developers to explore and test APIs easily.
- **Responsive Support**: Foster a culture of support and responsiveness to developer inquiries and issues.

Action Steps

- **Gather Feedback from Developers**: Regularly solicit feedback from API consumers to identify pain points and areas for improvement.
- **Invest in Developer Resources**: Create dedicated resources, such as tutorials, guides, and sample code, to enhance the developer experience.

Preparing for the future of RESTful APIs involves a proactive approach to development, security, and performance optimization. By embracing API-first design, investing in automation, focusing on security, leveraging emerging technologies, enhancing monitoring and analytics, and fostering a developer-centric culture, organizations can position themselves for success in the evolving landscape of API development.